THE ŚĀLISTAMBA SŪTRA

THE ŚĀLISTAMBA SŪTRA

Tibetan Original
Sanskrit Reconstruction
English Translation
Critical Notes
(including Pāli parallels,
Chinese version and ancient
Tibetan fragments)

N. Ross Reat

MOTILAL BANARSIDASS PUBLISHERS
PRIVATE LIMITED ● DELHI

First Edition: Delhi, 1993
Reprint: Delhi, 1998

ISBN: 81-208-1135-6

MOTILAL BANARSIDASS

41 U.A. Bungalow Road, Jawahar Nagar, Delhi 110 007
8 Mahalaxmi Chamber, Warden Road, Mumbai 400 026
120 Royapettah High Road, Mylapore, Chennai 600 004
Sanas Plaza, Subhash Nagar, Pune 411 002
16 St. Mark's Road, Bangalore 560 001
8 Camac Street, Calcutta 700 017
Ashok Rajpath, Patna 800 004
Chowk, Varanasi 221 001

PRINTED IN INDIA

BY JAINENDRA PRAKASH JAIN AT SHRI JAINENDRA PRESS,
A-45 NARAINA INDUSTRIAL AREA, PHASE I, NEW DELHI 110 028
AND PUBLISHED BY NARENDRA PRAKASH JAIN FOR
MOTILAL BANARSIDASS PUBLISHERS PRIVATE LIMITED,
BUNGALOW ROAD, DELHI 110 007

Dedicated to
Edward Conze

Contents

Acknowledgments ix
Preface xi

Introduction 1

Date and Historical Importance of the Sūtra 1
Organization and Content of the Sūtra 5
Structure and Development of the Sūtra 13
European Literature on the Sūtra 15
The Present Edition 16
Sources and Layout of the Present Edition 18
Synopsis of Textual Sources 21
Textual Symbols 23
Abbreviations 24

Texts and Translation 25

Acknowledgments

The work contained herein would have been impossible without the assistance of the following teachers and friends:

Tashi Paljor of Gemur, Lahul Spiti, H.P., India,
Jita Sain Negi of the Tibetan Institute in Saranath, U.P., India,
P.D. Premasiri of the University of Sri Lanka at Peradeniya,
Rod Bucknell of the University of Queensland, Australia, and
Peter Xiao of Beijing, China (formerly a student at Coe College, Iowa).

PREFACE

The present edition of the *Śālistamba Sūtra*, a Mahāyāna text of great antiquity, is likely to be controversial on two levels: the historical and the philological. On both levels, it participates in and contributes to a complex and often emotional debate regarding the characteristics of earliest Buddhism, the acceptability of even inquiring into earliest Buddhism, and the nature of the evidence which legitimately may be brought to bear upon these questions. In all these regards, current, discouraging trends in Buddhist historiography may be traced to the initially salubrious influence of the recently deceased Edward Conze. Professor Conze started out in the late 1950's as something of a lone crusader against the then widespread assumption that the Pāli *suttas* of Theravāda Buddhism contain the earliest, most faithful account of the teachings of the historical Buddha now available. Quite properly, Conze demanded proof of this assumption, and none has been forthcoming. Indeed, the pendulum has swung the other way, and now most modern scholars — particularly those in North America — have adopted wholeheartedly Conze's contention that in the absence of positive evidence we can conclude only that Theravāda and Mahāyāna versions of the historical Buddha's teachings are divergent, equally reliable records of a pre-canonical Buddhism which is now lost forever.

That there was some such pre-canonical Buddhism is beyond doubt. The mere writing down of an oral tradition itself constitutes a profound transformation, and there can be little doubt that further modifications in all of the various written traditions have occurred over the centuries. Nonetheless, the question remains as to whether or not, in general, the Pāli *suttas* reflect earliest Buddhism more faithfully than the *sūtra* literature of the Mahāyāna. The most natural conclusion — the conclusion reached by most of the pioneers of Buddhist studies in the West — is that the sober and coherent account preserved in the Pāli *suttas* predates significantly the exuberant, highly mythological account preserved in most Mahāyāna literature. Quite appropriately, Conze demanded evidence in support of this common sense conclusion. Inappropriately, many of his intellectual heirs now wish to rule out the possibility of such evidence. By providing evidence of precisely the sort that Conze demanded, the present publication seeks to re-open a debate prematurely closed by the safe but stifling historical agnosticism of the Conze school. It should therefore be controversial on a historiographical level. Such controversy is all the more likely because in the realm of scripture some scholars persist in equating "earlier" with "(religiously) more authoritative". This is particularly inappropriate in the context of Buddhism, in which it is axiomatic that "Whether or not Buddhas arise, the truth remains the same". Nonetheless, the preconscious conviction that "earlier" equates with "more authoritative" remains a source of misguided emotion in the field of Buddhist studies.

Due to the nature of the evidence adduced herein, the present publication should also be controversial on a philological level. Its methodology raises anew the question of what a "text" in fact is. The Sanskrit text contained herein is not copied from an old manuscript, much less from an inscription on an ancient stone dating back to the age of the historical Buddha. It is admittedly a modern construction which, as such, never before existed in space or time. In conventional terminology, it is a "reconstruction" of a lost Sanskrit text, a reconstruction based on an existing Tibetan text.

In the last two decades, the term "reconstruction" has acquired largely deserved, negative connotations in the realm of Buddhist studies. Too often, surviving Tibetan texts have simply been speculatively re-translated into Sanskrit. Too often again, the resulting Sanskrit text has been regarded as the primary text, in some cases even serving as the sole basis for translation into a modern language. This, of course, is sloppy procedure, and Tibetan oriented scholars have had every reason to complain about instances of it. Be that as it may, the present reconstruction does not seek to usurp the authoritativeness of any Tibetan text. It is, quite self-consciously, a modern construction, not an ancient text. It is not, however, merely a speculative retranslation of a Tibetan text into Sanskrit. Approximately 90% of the Sanskrit text included herein can be located in from one to four extant Sanskrit texts which claim to quote a Mahāyāna *sūtra* known as the *Śālistamba.* These extant Sanskrit texts represent different periods of history, and may well be based on different versions of the *Śālistamba Sūtra* available at the different times and places of their composition. For this reason alone, the Sanskrit text herein cannot be regarded as a resurrection of any single, ancient text. It is merely a justifiable reconstruction, an approximation encompassing several variant, ancient texts, each of which went under the name *Śālistamba Sūtra.*

Despite its possible defects, this reconstructed Sanskrit text is important for two reasons. Firstly, it serves to bring together all of the material which bears importantly upon the philological construal of the extant Tibetan texts of the *sūtra.* Of these there are several, preserved with very minor variations in the different editions of the Tibetan canon. This same material would need to be gathered and considered even if one did have an ancient Sanskrit manuscript of the *Śālistamba Sūtra* itself. This situation serves to highlight the artificiality of all scriptural texts, whether they are ancient manuscripts or modern, edited reconstructions. Virtually all available scriptural texts are redactions of yet earlier texts or oral traditions. Secondly, and much more importantly, the reconstructed Sanskrit text herein establishes objectively a defensible Sanskrit wording for about 90% of the extant Tibetan *sūtra.* This is particularly important in the present case for one, simple reason. It establishes beyond doubt that I did not simply fabricate a convenient Sanskrit rendition of the *Śālistamba Sūtra* as preserved in Tibetan.

Demonstrably, the Sanskrit text presented herein corresponds approximately to a text or texts of the *Śālistamba Sūtra* available to ancient Buddhist commentators. While admittedly the present edition does not reproduce any one of these ancient texts, demonstrably it corresponds closely enough so that relatively firm conclusions regarding parallel phrasing in extant Pāli texts may be reached. Such parallels in phrasing are of considerable historical importance. On the basis of the

Tibetan text of the *Śālistamba Sūtra* alone it is possible to demonstrate a surprising similarity between this Mahāyāna *sūtra* and extant Pāli *suttas*. The reconstructed Sanskrit text herein makes possible also the establishment of numerous direct or near direct parallels in phrasing between the ancient Mahāyāna text (or texts) and Theravāda *sutta* literature. According to the implicit position of the Conze school of Buddhist historiography — a position of entrenched historical agnosticism regarding earliest Buddhism — such similarities and parallels should not exist. They indicate that ancient and illustrious Mahāyāna scholars accepted as authoritative an entire *sūtra* which is in essence a Theravāda text in content and often even in precise phrasing. This situation constitutes at least circumstantial evidence for the common sense view that Mahāyāna Buddhism did indeed diverge gradually from a very early, commonly affirmed Buddhist tradition which is preserved more faithfully in the Pāli *suttas* of the Theravāda. To be sure, this evidence is not conclusive, but it may be augmented with further similar evidence derived from other apparently proto-Mahāyāna texts which contain Theravādin ideas and phrasing. The *Mahāvastu* (e.g. in the "Avalokita Sūtras") and the *Lalitavistara* contain such material, as do several texts in the Tibetan *Kanjur*, for example the texts on *pratītyasamtupāda* which immediately follow the *Śālistamba Sūtra*. For the time being, however, I hope that this no doubt defective, preliminary submission may serve to revive interest in the question of earliest Buddhism and in the important scholarly task of presenting the subsequent development of Buddhism as a comprehensible historical phenomenon.

INTRODUCTION

The *Śālistamba Sūtra* commands the attention of scholars of Buddhism for several reasons. It is one of the oldest Mahāyāna scriptures, probably composed, at least in its broad outlines, well before the beginning of the common era. Many passages in the *sūtra* have close parallels in the Pāli *suttas*. This suggests an even earlier date for much of the material in the *Śālistamba*, and throws considerable light upon the emergence of Mahāyāna Buddhism. The *Śālistamba* itself does not survive in Sanskrit, but it is the most quoted *sūtra* in Mahāyāna literature on the subject of *pratītyasamutpāda*. Many of the works which quote the *Śālistamba* extensively do survive in Sanskrit, which makes the *sūtra* an ideal candidate for reconstruction into Sanskrit. In all, about ninety per cent of the *sūtra* can be located in one, two, three or even four extant Sanskrit texts and matched against Tibetan and Chinese translations of the whole text.

There are four Chinese translations of the *Śālistamba Sūtra* (Taisho 709–712) which are in good general agreement with the standard Tibetan translation — "standard" in the sense that comparison of the Peking Narthang and Derge editions yields only minor variations. There is also a third century Chinese translation (Taisho 708) which is similar in content, but somewhat different in arrangement from the classical *Śālistamba*. This text throws some light on the possible development of the *sūtra* before it reached its final form. Finally, about half of the text survives in the form of manuscript fragments which are, along with the famous *rdo-ring* (pillar) inscription at the Jo Khang temple in Lhasa, the most ancient extant example of the Tibetan language. All of these situations combine to give the *Śālistamba Sūtra* considerable historical, textual and philological importance in the study of Buddhism. The present edition seeks to put under one cover all of the relevant textual material concerning this unique *sūtra*.

THE DATE AND HISTORICAL IMPORTANCE OF THE SŪTRA

External evidence establishes a relatively early date for the final composition of the *Śālistamba Sūtra*, but the content of the *sūtra* suggests far earlier origins. The most reliable date is established by the Chinese translation included in the table at the end of this introduction, Taisho 709. The introduction of this translation reveals that it was done in the Eastern Jin Dynasty (317–420 A.D.). The name of the translator is not given. As the table shows, this translation is in good general agreement with the contents of the standard Tibetan version, and is several centuries older.

An earlier Chinese translation, entitled *The Sūtra of Life and Death* (Taisho 708) was done in the Wu Dynasty (222–280 A.D.) by the grandson of the famous An Shigao, Ji Zhen, whose translating activities ran between 220 and 252 A.D.[1] A synopsis of this *sūtra* is given below. It agrees with the *Śālistamba* in overall organization and content, but includes some material in an order different from that in the Tibetan version. It also contains material not found in the Tibetan version or the surviving Sanskrit quotations of the *Śālistamba Sūtra*. Its terminology is non-standard, its style abrupt and obscure. Nonetheless it establishes beyond doubt that a *sūtra* very similar to the *Śālistamba* existed by about 250 A.D. For the *sūtra* to have gained acceptance as legitimate, it would have had to be regarded as ancient even at that time, which suggests a considerably earlier date, at least a hundred years earlier.

Three commentaries on the *Śālistamba Sūtra* which are attributed to Nāgārjuna survive in Tibetan (Peking nos. 5466, 5485, 5486). If any one of them really is his work, which is doubtful, it would push the date of the *sūtra* back further, depending on how one dates Nāgārjuna. Most commonly he is assigned to the second century. Again, though, the mere fact that commentaries on the *sūtra* are attributed to Nāgārjuna indicates that it has been regarded since early times as an ancient and venerable text.

The content of the *sūtra*, along with the many parallels in the Pāli canon, verifies and enhances this external evidence of the great antiquity of the *Śālistamba Sūtra*. Edward Conze has argued that where a close similarity can be established between Mahāsaṅghika material and the texts of the Theravādins and Sarvāstivādins, the date of agreeing passages should be fixed as prior to 340 B.C., the date he proposes for the council of Vesālī.[2] Many scholars would prefer the traditional one hundred years after the Buddha's death, i.e. *circa* 380 B.C. for the date of this council. At any rate, Conze seems to feel that such a process of dating is possible only regarding *Vinaya* material, noting that the Mahāsaṅghika version of the *sūtras* has been lost. The *Mahāvastu* and *Lalitavistara* may contain Mahāsaṅghika material, but most of the content is mythological and therefore uninformative regarding the nature of early doctrine. It would appear, however, that some of the material in the *Śālistamba Sūtra* satisfies Conze's criterion. It is some sort of early Mahāyāna work, even if not specifically Mahāsaṅghika, and it contains numerous, extensive parallels to Pāli *sutta* material.

This situation alleviates doubts raised by Conze and others concerning the accuracy of the Pāli *suttas'* account of the words of the historical Buddha. Conze argues that where the Theravāda and the Mahāyāna disagree upon the words of the Buddha, we are faced with divergent modifications of a precanonical Buddhism and cannot judge which is older. He implies as well that in no case may we imagine that we are dealing with the words of the historical Buddha himself, an aspiration which he deems "fruitless and impossible".[3]

The *Śālistamba* belies the certainty with which Conze's conclusion is stated. By Conze's own criteria some of the *Sūtra*'s content, namely that which closely parallels Pāli *sutta* passages, goes back to within a hundred years of the historical Buddha. There are no real reasons to doubt the Theravādin claim to have preserved a reasonably accurate and complete record of what the Buddha taught. The weak objections to this claim raised by Conze and others are further weakened by considering the evidence provided by the *Śālistamba Sūtra*.

The fact that the *Śālistamba* parallels the Pāli *suttas* extensively is persuasive evidence of great age, both of the *Śālistamba* and the Pāli *suttas*. It shows that ancient Mahāyāna Buddhists, perhaps the Mahāsaṅghikas, knew and accepted as authentic a version of the doctrine of *pratītyasamutpāda* which agrees in content and even exact phrasing with versions found in the Pāli *suttas*. Particularly noteworthy is the considerable similarity between the *Śālistamba* and the *Mahātaṇhā-saṅkhaya Sutta* (M1:256–71), and to a lesser extent the *Mahārā-hulovāda Sutta* (M1:420–26). There is no reason to doubt that if other Mahāyāna or Mahāsaṅghika texts from the time of the *Śālistamba* survived, they would contain similarly parallel, conservative material. In the absense of evidence to the contrary, the most reasonable conclusion is that the *Śālistamba Sūtra*, representing early Mahāyāna literature as a whole, is an elaboration upon yet earlier material which, in general, is recorded more accurately in the Pāli *suttas*.

Poussin remarked early on that there is nothing specifically Mahāyānist in the *Śālistamba*, other than that it is said to have been delivered by the Bodhisattva Maitreya, and that it concludes with a typically Mahāyāna passage.[4] This assessment is somewhat overstated, as will be discussed below, but it does serve to call attention to just how conservative the *Śālistamba Sūtra* is as a Mahāyāna text. Classification of the *sūtra* as a Mahāyāna work appears to be based more on its wide-spread acceptance by Mahāyānists than on the *sūtra's* contents. As noted above, it appears that the *sūtra* has enjoyed this wide-spread acceptance since very early times. The nature of the material in the *Śālistamba Sūtra* which does differentiate it from extant Theravāda material reinforces this conclusion.

Perhaps the most obviously Mahāyana characteristic of the *sūtra* is the centrality of the mythological figure Maitreya Bodhisattva, a figure who appears in the Pāli *suttas*, but not in such a prominent role (D3:76). In the *Śālistamba*, Maitreya fills the role played in the Pāli *suttas* by a number of the Buddha's chief disciples, the role of explicating the Buddha's remarks to junior monks. In the *Śālistamba Sūtra* Maitreya Bodhisattva is not portrayed as having any supernatural attributes whatsoever. His appearance as promulgator does not even give the writer the extra freedom of expression which might be afforded by a mythological protagonist. Instead, his role appears to be purely that of a marker to indicate that the compiler of the *Śālistamba* recognized that the *sūtra* departed from what was generally regarded as the accurate historical record at the time of compilation. In this connection, it is interesting that the oldest Chinese version, the *Sūtra of Life and Death*, does not mention Maitreya and attributes the *sūtra* instead to Sāriputra. There are other indications, which will be discussed below, that this translation may have been of an older version of the *Śālistamba* than that contained herein.

Less obviously but more crucially Mahāyāna content of the *Śālistamba* is the introductory material which reveals that the *sūtra* is essentially a discourse on the progressive realization of *Dharma-kāya* Buddha. In paragraph two, the *Śālistamba* says: "Whoever, monks, sees conditioned arising sees Dharma, and whoever sees Dharma sees the Buddha." The statement is incipiently Mahāyāna, but the terms are remarkably Theravādin. This passage is, in fact, a conflation of two well known passages from the Pāli *suttas* (M1:191 and S3:120). What is even more remarkable is that in paragraph seven, where it is specified that the deified Buddha is intended, the term used is *Dharma-śarīra*, rather than *Dharma-kāya*, the standard term. From paragraph seven on, it is clear that the *Śālistamba* expresses a fundamental Mahāyāna position, but it does so in remarkably conservative, even quaint terms.

This fundamental Mahāyana position—that enlightenment represents a realization of *Dharma-kāya* Buddha—is dealt with in the *sūtra* primarily in terms of a lengthy exposition of *pratītyasamutpāda*. Most of this material would not offend the sensibilities of an orthodox Theravādin, and much of it would not even be surprising. The Theravādin, however, would see in the *Śālistamba Sūtra* a definite tendency to consolidate material found scattered throughout the Pāli *suttas*. In some cases, such consolidation is itself tantamount to interpretation of the Pāli material. In other cases, the systematization which such consolidation entails requires doctrinal elaboration and even innovation. Thus, at least, would the *Śālistamba Sūtra* appear to a Theravādin who assumed that the Pāli texts are the most ancient and accurate record of the historical Buddha's teaching.

This premise appears to afford, overall, the most reasonable explanation for the nature and content of the *Śālistamba Sūtra*. This apparent process of consolidation, systematization, elaboration and innovation will be examined in detail in the following section of the introduction. Suffice it to say here, with regard to the date and importance of the *Śālistamba Sūtra*, that the foregoing suggests the following conclusions. The *Śālistamba* appears to be a very old Mahāyāna *sūtra*, one of the oldest, if not the oldest, in existence. Parts of it, those parts with Pāli parallels, date back at least to the council of Vesali, circa 350 B.C., if not back to the time of the historical Buddha himself.

At some point not too long after 350 B.C., though possibly before, this ancient material was organized into the unique format of the *Śālistamba Sūtra*, essentially a fourfold exposition of *pratītyasamutpāda*—objective causes and conditions; subjective causes and conditions—involving a simile of the growth of a seed. This could have happened within a generation or two of the Buddha's death, or even earlier. At any rate, at some point, presumably after the Mahāsaṅghika schism at Vesali around 350 B.C., this material was applied specifically to exposition of the Mahāyāna doctrine of progressive realization of *Dharma-kāya* Buddha. At this point, the *Śālistama Sūtra* as such was born. Other material may have been gradually added to the core text before or after this point of birth, but such revisions could not have continued long after 200 B.C. Beyond this point, Mahāyāna Buddhism had begun to develop a clear doctrinal direction, complete with terminological conventions. The *Śālistamba Sūtra* does not participate in these developments. By the end of the first century B.C. these developments had produced the earliest fully Mahāyāna texts, parts of the *Prajñāparamita* literature and *Lotus Sutra*. Clearly, developments in the *Śālistamba Sūtra* had ceased by that time. Otherwise it would be more obviously and typically Mahāyāna in content and expression. All this suggests, as the date of the *Sālistamba Sūtra* as a whole, 200 B.C. plus or minus 100 years.

The historical importance of the *Śālistamba Sūtra* is that it uniquely reveals, however dimly, a period in the development of Buddhist thought which would otherwise be accessible only to informed speculation. The early European scholars of Buddhism assumed, naturally and understandably, that the Pāli *suttas* recorded the earliest surviving form of Buddhism and that the various forms of Mahāyāna Buddhism had developed gradually from this simpler form of Buddhism. In this century, these pioneers have been severely, even vehemently taken to task for being less than historically rigorous in arriving at this premise.[5] The *Śālistamba sūtra* appears to redeem these pioneers to a considerable extent. Admittedly, some of the foregoing and some of what follows is somewhat speculative. Nonetheless, it deals with the only available material of its kind which bears directly upon a period of Buddhist history which is otherwise purely a subject of speculation and opinion. It reinforces what would appear to be, in the absense of positive evidence to the contrary, the most natural historical premise: that all forms of Buddhism developed divergently out of a primitive doctrine which is most faithfully recorded in the Pāli canon.

The extent to which the Pāli *suttas* accurately record the teachings of the Buddha himself may remain forever in doubt. The *Śālistamba Sūtra* does not decide this issue, but it does not discredit in any way the Theravādin claim accurately to record the historical Buddha's teachings. Only a very small amount of material in the *Śālistamba Sūtra* goes beyond the orthodox Theravādin position. This material is stated either by conflating statements actually found in the Pāli *suttas*, or in conservative terms which only hint at divergence from the orthodox Theravādin position. An example of the former is the *Śālistamba's* formulation of the progressive realization of *Dharma-kāya* Buddha by seeing *pratītyasamutpāda* and seeing Dharma. Examples of the latter are the similes of the reflected face and the reflected moon in paragraphs 36 and 37. These suggest the Mahāyāna doctrine of illusoriness, in terms not found in the Pāli *suttas*, but they are very conservative formulations. In fact, they cannot be recognized as deviations from the Theravādin position except in the light of later, more developed Mahāyāna doctrinal formulations.

From a Theravādin point of view, then, the *Śālistamba Sūtra* is composed of accepted material plus acceptable new material plus questionable, but ambiguous new material. If the *Śālistamba* is, as it appears to be, one of the earliest if not the earliest Mahāyāna *sūtra* in existence, this situation implies a genuine, gradual development from a primitive doctrine like the Theravāda to the various forms of Mahāyāna doctrine. Nothing in the *Śālistamba* suggests a precanonical Buddhism from which the Theravāda and Mahāyāna divergently developed. There may have been doctrinal formulations yet older than the Theravāda, but the *Śālistamba*, which appears to be the only *sūtra* in existence which might provide evidence for such formulations, provides none. In fact, it points to a gradual development from the Theravāda formulation to later formulations.

ORGANIZATION AND CONTENT OF THE SŪTRA

The basic organization of the *Śālistamba Sūtra* reveals an intent to consolidate and systematize material, much of which is found scattered through the Pāli *suttas*. For example, the distinction between objective and subjective phenomena is common in the Pāli *suttas*, as at M1:56, but it is not systematically treated, and in the Pāli *suttas*, *paṭiccasamuppāda* is treated only as a subjective, psychological process. The *Śālistamba*

Sūtra adopts as its basic organizational structure an objective and a subjective consideration of *pratītyasamutpāda*. It employs a simile of the development of a plant from a seed in its treatment of *pratītyasamutpāda* as an objective process. The Pāli *suttas* abound with seed and plant similes, as at D2:354 and S3:54, though these are not specifically plied to elucidating *paṭiccasamuppāda* and are not as botanically detailed as the simile in the *Śālistamba Sūtra*.

The *Śālistamba* achieves its fourfold organizational structure by considering cause (*hetu*) and condition (*pratyaya*) in relation to both objective and subjective *pratītyasamutpāda*. The Pāli *suttas* use *hetu* and *paccaya* interchangably, though a similar distinction between the terms appears in Pāli literature as early as the *Paṭṭhāna* of the *Abhidhamma*, which lists *hetu* as the first of its 24 *paccayas* (Pt.1:1). In other words, *hetu*, as the direct cause of an event, is a more specific term than *pratyaya*, which may also indicate any of the ancillary conditions necessary for the occurance of the event. The *Śālistamba Sūtra's* distinction between these terms is in basic agreement with this general distinction, but implies a more rigid differentiation between the terms by featuring them so prominently in its fourfold organization.

In pursuing the systematization implied in its fourfold organization, the *Śālistamba Sūtra* consolidates and systematizes relevant material scattered through the Pāli *suttas*. Attempting to make its systematization intelligible and persuasive, the *Śālistamba* does not shy away from elaborating upon more traditional definitions of terms. In some cases, such elaboration, and even the mere consolidation of apparently similar material, is tantamount to doctrinal innovation. As the *pratītyasamutpāda* formula as such never became very important in Mahāyāna Buddhism, many of the elaborations and innovations in the *Śālistamba Sūtra* appear to have had little impact beyond the *sūtra* itself. In some cases, however, there is a discernable drift from the orthodox Theravāda position toward what was eventually to become characteristic of Mahāyāna Buddhism.

Beyond its basic fourfold organization—objective and subjective *pratītyasamutpāda* considered from the viewpoints of causes and conditions—the most notable consolidation of material in the *Śālistamba* is the identification of *pratyayas* (conditions) with the six *dhātus* (factors). The term *dhātu* in the Pāli canon usually refers to the great elements (*mahābhūta*), or the six types of consciousness (*viññāṇa*) with their six organs and six objects (*āyatana*). Less commonly in the Pāli *suttas*, *dhātu* refers to the four great elements plus space and consciousness (e.g. D3: 247), as it does in the *Śālistamba*. In the Pāli *suttas*, these six *dhātus* are not specifically identified as being *pratyayas*, nor are they specifically applied to *paṭiccasamuppāda*, though the latter is perhaps implied at S3: 231, where these six *dhātus* are said to produce decay and death.

By construing the *dhātus* as it does, the *Śālistamba Sūtra* is able to consolidate and systematize a large amount of material. Even in the Pāli *suttas*, these *dhātus* are associated with specific "characteristics, functions and manifestations". These associations were expanded and systematized in the *Abhidhamma* and commentarial literature, as Tables I–IV indicate.

Analysis of the six (or five) *dhātus* in the *Śālistamba*, the Pāli *Suttas* and *Abhidhamma*, and Buddhaghosa's *Visuddhimagga*.

I. *Śālistamba* para. 24

DHĀTU	CHARACTERISTIC	FUNCTION	MANIFESTATION
Earth (*pṛthivī*)	solid (*kaṭhina*)	conglomeration (*saṁślesa*)	
Water (*ap*)		cohesion (*anuparigraha*)	
Heat (*tejas*)		digestion (*paripāka*)	
Wind (*vāyu*)		breathing (*āśvāsa-praśvāsa*)	
Space (*ākāśa*)		hollowness *śauṣīrya*)	
Consciousness (*vijñāna*)		development of name-and-form (*nāma-rūpa*)	

II. *Majjhima-nikāya: Mahā Rāhulovāda Sutta* (Vol. I, pp. 421–3)

DHĀTU	CHARACTERISTIC	FUNCTION	MANIFESTATION
Earth (*paṭhavī*)	hard (*kakkhaḷa*) solid (*kharigata*)		solid parts of the body
Water (*āpo*)	liquid, fluid (*āpo, āpogata*)		liquid parts of the body
Heat (*tejo*)	radiance, heat (*tejo, tejogata*)	digestion (*pariṇāma*)	body heat (*santappati, pariḍayhati*) maturing (*jīrīyati*)
Wind (*vāyo*)	windy (*vāyogata*)	breathing (*assāso-passāso*)	vital airs (*vātā*)
Space (*ākāsa*)	spacoius (*ākāsagata*)	room for food etc.	bodily cavities

III. ***Abhidhamma: Vibhaṅga*** **pp. 82–4 (internal,** ***ajjhattikā, dhātus)***

DHĀTU	CHARACTERISTIC	FUNCTION	MANIFESTATION
Earth (*paṭhavī*)	hard, solid (*kakkhaḷa*) (*kharigata*)		solid parts of the body
Water (*āpo*)	liquid, fluid (*āpo, āpogata*)	cohesion (*bandhanatta*)	liquid parts of the body
Heat (*tejo*)	heat, radiance (*tejo, tejogata*) warmth (*usmā, usmāgata*)	digestion (*pariṇāma*)	body heat (*santappati, pariḍayhati*) maturing (*jīrīyati*)
Wind (*vāyo*)	windy (*vāyo, vāyogata*)	breathing (*assāso-passāso*)	vital airs (*vātā*)
Space (*ākāsa*)	spacious (*ākāsagata*), non-resistant (*agha*), porous (*vivara*), untouchable (*asamphuṭṭha*)	room for food, etc.	bodily cavities
Consciousness (*viññāṇa*)			the six senses

IV. ***Visuddhimagga*** **pp. 365 & 448**

DHĀTU	CHARACTERISTIC	FUNCTION	MANIFESTATION
Earth (*paṭhavī*)	hardness (*kakkhaḷattā*)	foundation (*patiṭṭhāna*)	receiving (*sampaṭicchana*)
Water (*āpo*)	trickling (*paggharaṇa*)	intensifying (*brūhana*)	cohesion (*saṅgaha*)
Heat (*tejo*)	heat (*uṇhatta*)	maturing, digestion (*paripācana*)	softness (*maddava*)
Wind (*vāyo*)	distending (*vitthambhana*)	motion (*samudīraṇa*)	conveying (*abhinīhāra*)
Space (*ākāsa*)	delimiting forms (*rūpa-pariccheda*)	displaying the boundaries of form (*rūpa-pariyantappakāsana*	the confines of form (*rūpamariyādā*), untouchableness (*asamphuṭṭhabhava*), gaps and apertures (*chiddavivarabhava*)

Comparison of these treatments shows that the *Śālistamba Sūtra* has consolidated most of the pertinent material found in the other treatments insofar as *pratītyasamutpāda* is concerned. This is not to suggest that the compiler/s of the *Śālistamba* had direct access to any of these sources. It does indicate, however, that the compiler/s of the *sūtra* had access to developments in the *dhātu* theory beyond what is found in the Pāli *suttas*.

That these developments were eventually accepted in the Theravāda as well suggests that early Mahāyāna literature did not result from a radical doctrinal departure from the tradition recorded in the Pāli canon. Instead, the treatment of *dhātus* in the *Śālistamba* suggests gradual development of terms, concepts and formulations recorded in an earlier form in the Pāli *suttas*. Moreover, it suggests that in the early stages of its development, the movement which eventually resulted in Mahāyāna Buddhism was not self-consciously schismatic. Instead, it participated in a general movement within early Buddhism to systematize and elaborate ancient material into a more coherent and persuasive doctrine. It appears that the Theravāda, as well as the other schools of so called "Hīnayāna" Buddhism, chose to record such elaborations in the *Abhidhamma* and then the commentarial literature, whereas the originators of Mahāyāna Buddhism chose to incorporate them into the *sūtras* themselves. Such changes in the *sūtras* eventually led to the development of a body of literature which was not acceptable to more conservative Buddhists, partly because it deviated from what had come to be regarded as the authentic words of the Buddha, and partly because of new doctrines which began to appear in proto-Mahāyāna literature such as the *Śālistamba Sūtra*. Further examples of this apparent process of elaboration and gradual deviation appear in the balance of this section of the introduction.

In order to apply this set of *dhātus*, construed as *pratyayas* (conditions) in objective *pratītyasamutpāda*, the *Śālistamba Sūtra* replaces consciousness with *ṛtu* (season), since plants do not appear to be conscious. From the Theravāda point of view, this is an error, since *ṛtu* is not a *dhātu*. Interestingly, all of the Sanskrit sources of the *Śālistamba* avoid the technical error of calling *ṛtu* a *dhātu*, while the Tibetan is not so scrupulous in this regard. At any rate, by interpreting the *dhātus* as *pratyayas* and making this substitution, the *Śālistamba* systematizes and makes explicit the similarity between botanical rebirth and growth and the rebirth and growth of consciousness, a similarity which is implied in a number of Pāli *sutta* passages, e.g. S1:134, S3:54, D2:354 and A1:223, but is not explicitly treated. The latter three Pāli passages in particular draw comparisons similar to those found in paragraph 32 of the *Śālistamba*. Thus, the section on the "four limbs" of subjective *pratītyasamutpāda*, paragraphs 31 through 34, appear to serve the purpose of identifying the ancient material being elaborated and specifying the nature of the similarity between objective and subjective *pratītyasamutpāda* as systematized in the *Śālistamba Sūtra*.

Immediately following this section on the "four limbs" of subjective *pratītyasamutpāda* is a section on "five principals" (*kāraṇa*) of subjective *pratītyasamutpāda*, paragraphs 35 through 38. The translation "principals" is to distinguish this section from the immediately following section which deals with a different set of five *kāraṇas*, translated there more properly as "principles". Like the section on the "four limbs", the section on the "five principals" draws on material found in the Pāli canon. This section, however, draws conclusions from this material which not only deviate technically from the Theravāda position, but which reveal a clear drift toward the concerns and doctrines of Mahāyāna Buddhism.

This section opens with an enumeration of five conditions which must coincide for the occurance of visual consciousness. Similar, though not identical, lists of conditions occur throughout the Pāli *suttas*, e.g. M1:111 and 190. Such treatments in the Pāli *suttas* imply a somewhat skeptical attitude regarding the independent existence of an external, material world, but the Pāli *suttas*, as well as Theravāda Buddhism as a whole, do not propose a metaphysical doctrine of illusoriness. The *Śālistamba Sūtra* does not explicitly propose a metaphysical doctrine of illusoriness either. It comes only slightly closer to such a position than the following well known passage, which is a quotation by Buddhaghosa of some unspecified, traditional source, presumably Theravādin.

> There is suffering, but there is no sufferer,
> One finds the deed, but not a doer,
> There is nirvana, but no person who attains it,
> There is the path, but no traveler is found.
>
> *Vsm. p. 513*

Buddhaghosa in quoting this passage, like the *Śālistamba Sūtra* in the section under consideration, is elaborating on the doctrine of *anātman*. The *Śālistamba*, however, goes somewhat beyond the position in Buddhaghosa's quotation by including the term illusion (*māyā*), albeit ambiguously, in paragraph 38. More importantly, it employs in paragraphs 36 and 37 similes of reflected images (*pratibimba*), which became important as illustrations of illusoriness in later Mahāyāna texts, e.g. the *Ratnāvalī, Pañcaviṁśatisāhasrikā*, and *Laṅkāvatāra Sūtras*.[6]

Following the sections on the "four limbs" and the "five principals", which occur only in the *sūtra's* treatment of subjective *pratītya-samutpāda*, is a section on the "five principles" (*kāraṇa*), paragraphs 39 through 44, which is paralleled in the objective section in paragraphs 15 through 20. The material in these sections has no parallels in the Pāli *suttas*, other than the rejection of eternalism (*sassatavāda*) and annihilationism (*ucchedavāda*), as at S4:400. These sections appear to record material that developed in the course of refuting errant interpretations and criticisms of the Buddhist concept of rebirth.

The concluding section of the *sūtra*, paragraphs 45–48, is Mahāyāna in the impression it conveys more than in content. The only specifically Mahāyāna content of this section is the prediction of complete Buddhahood in paragraph 47, which occurs only in the Tibetan and Chinese translations. The rhetorical flourish in paragraph 45, which is paralleled in paragraph 7, has something of a Mahāyāna flavor, but none of the long string of adjectives would be objectionable from a Theravāda point of view. Contrary to what Poussin seems to think,[7] the mythological beings said to have been in attendance at Maitreya's discourse in paragraph 48 of the Tibetan version, as well as some Chinese versions, are not exclusively Mahāyāna characters. Similar beings populate the Pāli *suttas*, as at D3:76.

The core of the *Śālistamba Sūtra* is its elaboration upon cause (*hetu*) in the subjective *pratītyasamutpāda* formula. Each section of this treatment consolidates a considerable amount of material, much of which can be located in a similar though less systematic form in the Pāli *suttas*.

In addition to the standard twelvefold enumeration of *paṭiccasamuppāda* in the Pāli *suttas*, there occur shorter lists of ten or even nine items, as at D2:32 and D2:56 respectively. In fact, the entire twelvefold enumeration of the *paṭiccasamuppāda* formula is not listed anywhere in the *Dīgha-nikāya*.[8] The *Dīgha-nikāya* also contains a set of nine causes and results which are entirely different from the standard *paṭiccasamuppāda* formula, but are dealt with using the standard connective phrases of *paṭiccasamuppāda* (D2:58–62). Considerations such as these suggest that the standard, twelvefold *paṭiccasamuppāda* formula developed over a period of time, though possibly within the Buddha's lifetime, as a result of consolidation of various cause and effect relationships which formed part of very early Buddhist doctrine. As a result, the precise meaning of the formula as it occurs in the Pāli *suttas* is unclear. Ninian Smart, for example, suggests that it is actually a combination of three separate formulas, ignorance and mental formations dealing with rebirth, the terms from consciousness to sensations dealing with everyday psychological phenomena, and the terms from craving to decay and death being an elucidation of the first two noble truths.[9]

In paragraphs 27–29 the *Śālistamba Sūtra* attempts to rectify this lack of clarity in the formula by making more explicit the causal connections between adjacent items in the series. This attempt is made largely with recourse, again, either to consolidation of material available in the Pāli *suttas* or to incorporation of conservative material which is not, in itself, objectionable from the Theravāda point of view. The overall effect of this treatment of *pratītyasamutpāda* is, however, a general drift in the direction of the concerns of the Mahāyāna.

In the Pāli *suttas*, ignorance is defined almost exclusively as doctrinal ignorance of the four noble truths. There are exceptions, such as at A2: 10, where it is ignorance of the arising of the six sense entrances (*āyatana*) and escape therefrom. The *Śālistamba* defines ignorance more as a perceptual flaw than an intellectual misapprehension. In so doing, it incorporates some terms which may be reactions to the doctrines of opponent schools which arose after the time of the historical Buddha, for example, the *ahaṁkāra* of Sāṁkhya or the *pudgala* of the Pudgalavādins.

The *Śālistamba* elaborates upon the *sutta* definition of mental formations by incorporating the three "roots of unwholesomeness" (*akusalamūla*) and the three *abhisankhāras* (*puñña, apuñña, āṇeñja*). This allows consciousness to be more convincingly related to mental formations than in the Pāli *suttas*, where consciousness is normally defined merely as being of six types, i.e. the five senses and mind. The *suttas* normally define mental formations, in the context of *paṭiccasamuppāda*, as the three types of karma, bodily, vocal and mental. The alternative meaning of *sankhāra* in the *suttas*, conceptualization of phenomena, complicates further the issue of the nature of the relationship between consciousness and mental formations. The *Śālistamba Sūtra* clarifies this relationship by implying that *saṁskāra* is to be understood as the habitual karmic propensities of the individual, and that this quality influences the individual's perceptual consciousness, the way in which the world is experienced. This implication helps to overcome one of the "weak links" in the chain of *pratītyasamutpāda* which Smart has noted. It also gives the *Śālistamba Sūtra's* treatment of *pratītyasamutpāda* a Mahāyāna flavor by maintaining its perceptual slant and implying more directly than the Pāli *suttas* that the nature of the world is a function of the nature of one's mind, i.e., that reality as such is illusory, a product of one's mind.

The *Śālistamba's* treatment of name and form (*nāma-rūpa*) is of great interest in the history of Buddhist doctrine. It defines name as the four nonmaterial aggregates, and form as the four great elements. This eventually came to be the accepted definition of the term in the Theravāda, though even Buddhaghosa is reluctant to state this definition explicitly, and only hints at in a roundabout fashion, as at Vsm. pp. 438–9. The standard *sutta* definition of *nāma* is that it is comprised of *vedanā, saññā, cetanā, phassa,* and *manasikāra*. Normally, Buddhaghosa defines *nāma* as *vedanā, saññā* and *sankhārā*, as at Vsm. p. 558.

Having defined name and form as mind and body, and having thus departed from the *sutta* definition of the term, as did the later Theravādins, the *Śālistamba* can imply that the next link in the chain, the six sense spheres, is to be understood as the development of the mental and physical aspects of the senses. Furthermore, again maintaining its perceptual slant, the *Śālistamba* suggests that this development of the senses will determine the type of contact (*sparśa*) one will have with one's environment. The next link in the chain, sensation (*vedanā*) is then said to be "the experience of contact", again suggesting the doctrine of illusoriness, in that the nature of reality is portrayed as depending upon one's perception or experience, which is determined not by an external reality, but by one's mental predispositions, which are in turn determined by past karma. This implication, though discernable, is far less evident in the Pāli *suttas*, which define the senses and contact merely by enumerating the six senses and the similar six types of sensory contact, and define sensation as being of three types, pleasant, unpleasant and neutral.

In the Pāli *suttas*, desire (*taṇhā*) is defined as being of three types, desire for sensual pleasure, for existence and for nonexistence. Therein, grasping (*upādana*) is defined as being of four types, grasping after sensual pleasure, speculative views, rites and rituals and belief in a soul. The *Śālistamba*, by contrast, maintains more continuity with previous terms in the chain, thereby maintaining its implication that *pratītyasamutpāda* describes an essentially illusory world. Desire and grasping are portrayed as relating to sensations pure and simple, not, as in the Pāli *suttas*, to pleasure, existential status or abstract beliefs and practices. The *Śālistamba's* treatment of the next link, becoming (*bhava*), again establishes more continuity in the formula by defining becoming as action (*karma*) and noting that action is a result of grasping, presumably grasping after mere sensations. The Pāli *suttas* define becoming as being of three types, *kāma-bhava, rūpa-bhava* and *arūpa-bhava*, i.e. the three realms in which rebirth is thought to be possible, the realms of desire, fine materiality and non-materiality. They do not explain how these result from grasping.

By defining mental formations (*sankhāra*) as corresponding to the three types of action (*kamma*), bodily, vocal and mental, Pāli treatments of *paṭiccasamuppāda* seem to suggest that rebirth is represented twice in the formula, once when mental formations condition consciousness (*viññāṇa*) and again when becoming (*bhāva*) conditions birth (*jāti*). This has resulted in the Theravāda interpretation of the formula as describing parts of three lifetimes: the end of one, when ignorance conditions a final, volitional thought (*sankhāra*); the beginning of a second, when consciousness is established in a womb as a result of this volitional thought and proceeds to exist (*bhava*) by way of a repetitive conditioned arising of the eight links between consciousness and becoming; and a third life described only briefly as comprising birth, decay and death (Vsm. 578). The *Śālistamba Sūtra* by contrast, appears to interpret the ten links preceding birth as being pre-natal developments resulting in the appearance of a fully formed individual comprised of five aggregates and permeated with desire and grasping. The aggregates thus born mature, decay and eventually perish, deluded and attached (para. 27), i.e. ignorant, and the chain begins again, in another rebirth.

In these ways, the *Śālistamba Sūtra* consolidates, systematizes and clarifies much essentially conservative Buddhist material, much of which can be located in the Pāli *suttas*. In so doing, however, it drifts discernably in the direction of a doctrine of illusoriness. This drift, in conjunction with the overtly Mahāyāna material mentioned in the previous section, justifies its classification as a Mahāyāna *sūtra*. As such, the *sūtra* as a whole suggests that the development of Mahāyāna literature, in its early stages, was a gradual, unselfconscious process based on an attempt to consolidate, systematize and clarify ancient, conservative material, much of which can be located in the Pāli *suttas*, and most of which, in and of itself, does not contradict the orthodox, Theravādin point of view.

This situation tends to verify the Theravāda's claim to be the direct descendants of the Sthavīravāda and thus to possess the most ancient surviving record of the teachings of the historical Buddha. It also suggests that in the early stages of its development Mahāyāna Buddhism recognized the authority of this ancient scriptural tradition, and only gradually began to claim historical accuracy for its own scriptures.

STRUCTURE AND POSSIBLE DEVELOPMENT OF THE SŪTRA

Paragraph 10 of the *Śālistamba* sets up the basic fourfold organization of the *sūtra*: objective and subjective *pratītyasamutpāda* considered from the standpoints of cause (*hetu*) and condition (*pratyaya*). Paragraphs 11 through 14 consider the causes and conditions operative in objective *pratītyasamutpāda*, and are paralleled by paragraphs 22 through 25 in the subjective section, with paragraph 21 reiterating the organizational scheme set out in paragraph 10. Paragraphs 15 through 20 in the objective section parallel paragraphs 39 through 44 in the subjective section, considering respectively the so called five principles of objective and subjective *pratītyasamutpāda*. Thus, paragraphs 10–20 of the objective section, and their parallels, paragraphs 21–25/39–44 may be regarded as the most basic content of the *sūtra*.

Paragraphs 1 through 9 form an introduction and paragraphs 45 through 48 a conclusion. Paragraphs 26 through 38 interject material which destroys the symmetry of the *sūtra*. It is perhaps notable that most of the Mahāyāna content of the *sūtra* occurs in these paragraphs, i.e., the introduction, the conclusion and the interjection. It is also interesting that Sanskrit sources are least available for the introductory and concluding portions of the *sūtra*, as is clear in the Synopsis of Textual Sources which follows this introduction.

Furthermore, the most ancient Chinese translation, the *Sūtra of Life and Death* deviates most significantly from other versions of the *Sālistamba Sūtra* with regard to the interjected paragraphs 26 through 38. It omits paragraphs 3 through 9, and contains a variant ending after paragraph 44. Its contents may be summarized as follows (numbers indicate paragraphs; slashes indicate breaks): 2/10–22/digression/23–24/26–33/36/38/37/digression/35 variant/one sentence of 34/39–44/variant conclusion/. This might indicate that its translator had in hand a more ancient version of the *sūtra* than survives otherwise. Its translator, Ji Zhen, was a member of the Yue-zhi, or Scythian people who inhabited the northwestern trade routes through which Buddhism entered China, and along which Buddhism was established before entering China. Between 220 and 252, when he was active as a translator,[10] he may have had access to a more ancient text than was available to later Chinese and Tibetan translators, or even to the Indian commentators who quoted the *Śālistamba Sūtra*.

Be that as it may, all translations of the *sūtra* agree that it was occasioned by the Buddha contemplating a stalk of rice (*śālistamba*), and that its basic organization is a fourfold consideration of causes and conditions as they relate to objective and subjective *pratītyasamutpāda*.

All these considerations suggest the following conclusions, admittedly tentative, regarding the development of the *sūtra*. At a relatively early date, the basic, fourfold content of the *sūtra* — paragraphs 10–25/39–44 — was associated with the material in paragraph 2, which names the *sūtra*, introduces the botanical treatment of objective *pratī tyasamutpāda*, and conflates the two statements: "Whoever sees *pratītyasamutpāda* sees Dharma" and "Whoever sees Dharma sees the Buddha". Aside from the appearance of Maitreya Bodhisattva, the introductory material in paragraphs 1 and 3 through 9 is very conservative in form and content, and therefore might also represent some of the most ancient content of the *sūtra*. Of this basic material, paragraphs 15 through 20 and 39 through 44, on the "four limbs" of objective and subjective *pratītyasamutpāda*, which have no real parallels in the Pāli *suttas*, might represent a relatively early addition to the basic *sūtra*. Paragraph 26 is closely related to paragraph 25, and would not be expected to be paralleled by a similar paragraph concerning plants. This paragraph too might therefore be a relatively early addition or part of the original content of the *sūtra*.

The remaining material in the *Śālistamba Sūtra* would appear to have been added at a later date or dates in the following blocks: paragraphs 27 through 29, which elaborate upon the twelve links in the *pratītyasamutpāda* formula and imply illusoriness; paragraphs 30–34, which treat the "four limbs" of subjective *pratītyasamutpāda*; paragraphs 35 through 38, which discuss the "five principals" of subjective *pratītyasamutpāda*; and the concluding paragraphs 45 through 48.

To repeat, all of these additions are likely to have occurred before 100 B.C., otherwise, one would expect more selfconsciously Mahāyāna material. All in all, the content of the *Śālistamba Sūtra* suggests a gradual scriptural development in Buddhism, which may have started during the Buddha's life or shortly thereafter, and which eventually resulted in an incompatability of doctrine and scriptural tradition between "conservative" and "liberal" Buddhists. The Mahāsaṅghika schism itself may have been precipitated by disciplinary disputes, as the Theravāda sources record, or by perceived spirital inadequacies in the elders (*sthavīras* or *theras*), as the Mahāyāna sources record. Be that as it may, the material in the *Śālistamba Sūtra* suggests that this schism was the result of a gradual divergence of scriptural remembrance and doctrinal understanding of the original teachings of the Buddha. Its existence belies claims that the Mahāyāna *sūtras* as a whole accurately record the words of the historical Buddha, or that they derive from a pre-canonical tradition significantly different from the tradition recorded in the Pāli *suttas*.

EUROPEAN LITERATURE ON THE SŪTRA

The significance of the *Śālistamba Sūtra* has not been altogether lost upon the European scholarly community, though it has received little attention in Western circles since its appearance early in this century. Considerable excitement greeted the initial discovery of Tibetan fragments of the *sūtra* among the finds from excavations in Chinese Turkestan lodged by M. Aurel Stein with the British Museum in the summer of 1902.[11] Shortly afterward, L.D. Barnett announced in the *Journal of the Royal Asiatic Society* that these fragments were the "earliest known relics of Tibetan literature", and predicted, "A new page of history is opening before us".[12] Cecil Bendall reports, in a note subjoined to Barnett's article, that L. de la Vallée Poussin was already editing a Sanskrit reconstruction of the same sūtra.[13] W.W. Rockhill and Barnett exchanged some rather huffy, but otherwise uninteresting correspondence concerning their disagreements over the importance of the *sūtra* in subsequent issues of the *JRAS*.[14] Stein finally published his *Ancient Khotan* in 1907.[15] Volume II of this work contained a reconstruction in Roman script, by Barnett, of the Stein fragments of the *Śālistamba Sūtra*. In all, about half of the original text of the ancient Tibetan manuscript was pieced together.

In 1913, Poussin published his promised reconstruction of the *Śālistamba Sūtra* under the title *Théorie des douze causes*.[16] It contains an introductory essay on the subject of *pratītyasamutpāda*, a reconstructed Sanskrit text of the *sūtra*, and a Tibetan text of the *sūtra* from an unidentified edition of the *Kanjur*, apparently the Narthang. He also includes in appendices several other Sanskrit and Tibetan texts and excerpts relevant to *pratītyasamutpāda*, taken from both Buddhist and Brahmanic sources. Poussin notes most of the important textual variations found in the several extant Sanskrit texts which quote portions of the *Śālistamba Sūtra*, namely the *Abhidharmakośa-sputhārtha*, *Bodhicaryāvatāra-pañjikā*, *Mādhyamaka-kārikā-prasannapadā*, the *Śikṣāsamuccaya*, and the *Bhāmatī*. He also notes variant Tibetan forms found in the Stein fragments as well as some passages from Pāli sources which parallel the reconstructed Sanskrit text. It is a pity that Poussin's thorough, learned and informative work has been out of print for several decades.

In 1950, N. Aiyaswami Sastri published another Tibetan text and Sanskrit reconstruction of the *Śālistamba Sūtra*,[17] but without consulting

Poussin's important work or noting the Stein fragments. Sastri's volume is somewhat difficult to obtain, but his reconstruction of the *Śālistamba* has been reprinted in volume 17 of the *Buddhist Sanskrit Texts* series.[18] This reprinting, however, omits all of the critical notes in Sastri's original edition, and still fails to take into account the Stein fragments or Poussin's generally superior edition.

This same volume of *Buddhist Sanskrit Texts* contains an edition by V.V. Gokhale of a 16th century Sanskrit manuscript containing most of the material in the *Śālistamba Sūtra*, as well as some clearly extraneous Mādhyamika material. Gokhale therefore labels his text, which he obtained in 1948–50 in Lhasa, the *Mādhyamaka-Śālistambasūtra*. It appears, though, that this text is itself a somewhat careless reconstruction of the *Śālistamba Sūtra* based on the *Bodhicaryāvatāra-pañjikā* for paragraphs 8 to 26 of the present edition, and the *Śikṣāsammuccaya* for paragraphs 27 to 45. Aside from the clearly extraneous Mādhyamika material, it contains nothing of the *Śālistamba Sūtra* not found in these two texts. Moreover, it contains only that material found in the *Bodhicaryāvatara-pañjika's* long, running quotation of the *Śālistamba*, omitting considerable material found elsewhere in the same text. A quick examination of the Synopsis of Textual Sources below will reveal the apparent reliance of the *Mādhyamika-Śālistambasūtra* on these two texts, as well as its apparent carelessness in employing them. (See, for example, para. 30 n.3 and para. 35 n.8.) Nonetheless, if it is indeed an early attempt at reconstruction of a *sūtra*, it is a remarkable document for just that reason. Be that as it may, Gokhale's edition does take into account Poussin's work on the *sūtra*. This is appreciated, but less helpful than it would have been if he had been working with a more complete version of the *Śālistamba*.

Thus, though the *Śālistamba Sūtra* has by no means been neglected, it has received uneven attention, so that this new edition, incorporating for the first time all available material of direct relevance to the *sūtra*, may prove useful, especially since Poussin's and Sastri's monographs are both difficult to obtain and do not contain translations of the *sūtra*.

THE PRESENT EDITION

This English version of the *Śālistamba Sūtra* is a translation of the Sanskrit reconstruction contained herein, a procedure which demands justification, given that the entire *sūtra* survives only in Tibetan and Chinese translations. This situation would normally imply that the Tibetan text would be the best source for an English translation of the *sūtra*. In this specific case, however, the text in question has been extensively quoted in several reliable and extant Sanskrit texts. In all, about ninety percent of the *sūtra* survives in Sanskrit. Using the complete Tibetan text as a guide, these quotations may be pieced together and edited critically to create a genuine "reconstruction" of the Sanskrit text rather than, as is often the case, merely a speculative Sanskrit translation of a Tibetan translation.

Even under such favorable circumstances, it must be remembered that the present translation does not refer back to any single original source. To emphasize this situation, I have enclosed in square brackets those parts of the Sanskrit and English texts which have no basis in an extant

Sanskrit source, i.e. which are retranslated from Tibetan. In the few cases in which the Sanskrit quotations of the *sūtra* contain more material that is implied in the Tibetan version, I enclose the words in question in parentheses in the Sanskrit reconstruction, and in parentheses followed by an asterisk — ( )* — in the English translation. Simple parentheses in the English translation indicate clarifying material with no counterpart in Sanskrit or Tibetan. These measures, hopefully, will serve as sufficient notice of the less than ideal circumstances of the present translation, and satisfy those who object, justifiably and correctly, to merely translating into Sanskrit texts which survive only in Tibetan and then regarding the Sanskrit "reconstruction" as the most authoritative text.

In this regard, I did consider leaving the few passages without Sanskrit sources in Tibetan, but this seemed pointless since the Tibetan text is included herein anyway. While admitedly these retranslated Sanskrit passages add nothing to our knowledge of the original Sanskrit text, they do at least indicate something about how the present translator has understood the Tibetan text, something which might not be as clear given the English translation alone. Having the *sūtra* run from beginning to end in Sanskrit will also be appreciated by those who do not read Tibetan. Moreover, as with all Tibetan translations of Sanskrit, consideration of the probable wording of the Sanskrit original is indespensible for scholarly comprehension and proper translation. Much of the vocabulary employed by the ancient Tibetan translators was artifically concocted specifically to render Buddhist terms into Tibetan. The translators themselves, without a doubt, thought largely in terms of Sanskrit. For the purposes of scholarly translation of Tibetan, the probable Sanskrit equivalents of technical terms are never irrelevant. Such probable equivalents, of course, need not dictate the wording of the translation, but they should be considered, and in important contexts, footnoted.

The basic policy adopted in the present translation is as follows. Where the Tibetan translation is the only source, the English agrees with it, and the speculative Sanskrit reconstruction is regarded as having only the status of a footnote. Where, as in ninety percent of the text, there is a Sanskrit source, it is, in general, preferred for two reasons. First, mistakes within one language are less likely than mistakes involving two languages. Second, the Indian writers almost certainly had older texts of the *sūtra* than the Tibetan translators.

This English translation is, then, a translation of the best version of the *sūtra* that I was able to reconstruct from the several sources available. Obviously, this involved a measure of judgement which, admittedly, may have been faulty. Scholars who are in a position to exercise similar judgement will find herein all the information necessary to do so. Those who are not in such a position may at least be aware where I have exercised judgement, and will probably appreciate having the best readings always in the text rather than sometimes in the critical apparatus, as would have been the case if I had translated from the Tibetan text alone.

Hopefully, this text will be useful to students of Sanskrit and Tibetan. For this reason, and to facilitate typesetting, continuously written Sanskrit phrases are broken where possible by hyphens. Also for purposes of typesetting, Sanskrit words are hyphenated at the end of a line after any vowel, as in the Devanāgarī script. The critical apparatus is fullish to facilitate use by beginners. In the Sanskrit text, unless otherwise specified, numbers at the end of a single word refer to that word alone; numbers at the end of a string of hyphenated words refer to the whole string or the last word in the string; and numbers after a punctuation slash refer to the whole sentence thus punctuated. In the notes themselves, parentheses enclose the next word in the text beyond the number which marks the note in cases where this might be in doubt otherwise.

SOURCES AND LAYOUT OF THE PRESENT EDITION

The following edition of the *Śālistamba Sūtra* is laid out in four sections for each paragraph. These are: English translation, Sanskrit reconstruction, Tibetan original, and notes. The core of the present edition is the standard Tibetan version of the *Śālistamba* found in the *Kanjur*. The Derge, Narthang and the Peking editions differ only very slightly in minor details in their respective versions of this *sūtra*. The Tibetan text herein follows the Peking edition without noting minor variations in the Narthang and Derge editions.

At the head of each paragraph of Sanskrit text is a list of the Sanskrit sources, in descending order of preference, employed in reconstructing that particular paragraph. Page numbers refer to the editions listed in the "abbreviations" section. Notes in the text indicate any variation from the preferred source in any of the other sources consulted. Occasionally, I have chosen a reading from other than the preferred source, but in any case, by consulting the notes, the version of the *Śālistamba Sūtra* appearing in any one of these sources may be reconstructed in full. The few sections of Sanskrit which have been reconstructed solely on the basis of the Tibetan, without recourse to an extant Sanskrit text, are enclosed in square brackets. Parentheses in the Sanskrit text enclose extant Sanskrit material for which there is no Tibetan equivalent. When the Tibetan seems to suggest a Sanskrit term which differs from that found in the Sanskrit sources, this is indicated in the notes with the probable Sanskrit of the Tibetan which does occur.

At the head of each paragraph is an English translation of the *sūtra*. In effect, this is a translation of the reconstructed Sanskrit text. Care has been taken, though, to indicate any material in the translation which deviates from the Tibetan version of the *sūtra*. In the English translation, square brackets enclose material for which there is no Sanskrit source, but which exists in the Tibetan text. Plain parentheses enclose words not found in Sanskrit or Tibetan, but merely inserted to clarify the English translation, e.g. "(sensory) contact" for *sparśa*. Parentheses followed by an asterisk — ( )* — enclose material for which there is no Tibetan equivalent, but which is found in at least one Sanskrit source. In the English text, the most certain content of the *sūtra*, that found in both Tibetan and Sanskrit, is unmarked. Material in square brackets, in general, is next to this in reliability, followed by material enclosed with parentheses and an asterisk. Material in plain parentheses has no credentials at all, and is merely to clarify the English.

Also in the English translation are notes which refer to the Chinese translation of the *Śālistamba Sūtra* which most closely agrees with the Tibetan translation, Taisho 709, written in the Eastern Jin Dynasty, 317–420 A.D. It is the second oldest of the Chinese translations. Because of the nature of the Chinese language, it is impossible to detect many minor terminological variations, but I have indicated where it appears that the Chinese translator may have had before him a different Sanskrit text than that used by the Tibetan translator. Some of these variants, of course, might be instances of intentional deviation from the Sanskrit text, or merely bad translation.

At the end of each paragraph are notes on the English, Sanskrit and Tibetan texts of the *sūtra.* They are numbered consecutively, starting over in each paragraph. Following these numbered notes, material from the Pāli *suttas* which closely parallels material in that paragraph is quoted in full, along with at least one reference in parentheses to a location in the *suttas*, though there may be many similar Pāli passages in some cases. Following the Pāli, any Stein fragments of the ancient Tibetan version of the paragraph in question are also reproduced in full. These follow Barnett's reconstruction. Any breaks in the text of these fragments are indicated by three dots. Parentheses enclose the probable contents of short breaks in the text. Where the Stein fragments or the Pāli parallels seemed relevant to the construal of the text, these are mentioned in numbered notes in addition to being quoted in full at the end of the notes for the section in question.

Following this introduction is a rough tabular summary, arranged by paragraphs, of the textual sources considered in the present edition. The abbreviations labeling the vertical columns are explained in the abbreviations section at the end of this introduction. The far left column, labeled "para.", gives the paragraph numbers of the present edition. A slash or an x in a given column indicates that the text in that column contains part or all of the paragraph in question. Because the *Bodhicaryāvatāra-pañjikā* quotes different sections of the *Śālistamba Sūtra* in three different places — pp. 386–87; 576–79; 480–83 — an a, b or c respectively is affixed to the x, indicating the occurrence of the paragraph in question on one of those three groups of pages. Otherwise, an x indicates the inclusion of the entire or almost entire paragraph on the pages cited at the head of each paragraph. A slash indicates partial inclusion, generally less than half. In the case of the Chinese, this estimate is often somewhat impressionistic, and a slash indicates that the Chinese is so far removed from the Tibetan that one may suspect a variant in the Sanskrit texts used by the translators rather than merely quirks or carelessness in translation. The column labeled Pāli gives the location of one parallel passage. Where two passages are given, different parts of the paragraph in question are paralleled at different locations in the Pāli canon. This table shows graphically how much material is available for a reconstruction of the *Śālistamba Sūtra.* Only three short paragraphs (5,6 and 47) lack any Sanskrit source. Two of these have Pāli parallels, and are in fact largely comprised of formulaic material well known in Buddhist literature in general. Aside from these, all but the first and last paragraphs are directly and substantially quoted in an extant Sanskrit source. Though the Pāli sources listed often do not contain parallels to whole paragraphs of the *Śālistamba*, this table also illustrates the extent of the *sūtra's* similarity to Pāli material.

Notes to Introduction

1. E. Zurcher, *The Buddhist Conquest of China*, Brill, Leiden, 1959, pp. 23–4, 50, 61.
2. Edward Conze, *Buddhist Thought in India*, Allen and Unwin, London, 1962, p. 31.
3. Ibid., pp. 31–2. See also, Conze, "Recent Progress in Buddhist Studies", *The Middle Way*, 34, 1959, pp. 6–14; reprinted in *Thirty Years of Buddhist Studies*, Cassirer, Oxford, 1967, pp. 1–32.
4. L. de la Vallée Poussin, *Théorie des douze causes*, Luzac, London, 1913, p. 69.
5. See G.D. Bond, "Theravada Buddhism and the Aims of Buddhist Studies", *Studies in the History of Buddhism*, ed. A.K. Narain, B.R. Publishing, Delhi, 1980, pp. 43–65, for a consideration and refutation of these criticisms.
6. *Ratnāvalī* I, 31–34, in *JRAS*, 1934, pp. 314–15; *Pañcaviṁśatisāhasrikā*, ed. N. Dutt, 1934, pp. 153–54; both quoted in *Buddhist Texts Through the Ages*, ed. E. Conze, Cassirer, Oxford, 1954, pp. 167 and 178. Laṅkāvatāra Sūtra, ed. Bunyu Nanjio, Otani Univ. Press, Kyoto, 1934, p. 353; D.T. Suzuki translation, Routledge and Kegan Paul, London, 1932, p. 278.
7. *Théorie des douze causes*, p. 69.
8. T.W. Rhys Davids, *Dialogues of the Buddha* (tsl. of *Dīgha Nikāya*), pt. 2, SBB vol. 4, 5th ed., Luzac, London, 1966, p. 42.
9. Ninian Smart, *Doctrine and Argument in Indian Philosophy*, Allen and Unwin, London, 1964, p. 46.
10. Zurcher, as note 1 above.
11. L.D. Barnett, "Preliminary Notice of the Tibetan Manuscripts in the Stein Collection", *Journal of the Royal Asiatic Society*, Jan. 1903, pp. 109–14.
12. ibid., pp. 109 and 113.
13. ibid., p. 113.
14. W.W. Rockhill, "Tibetan Mss. in the Stein Collection", *JRAS*, July 1903, pp. 572–75. L.D. Barnett, "Tibetan Mss. in the Stein Collection", *JRAS*, Oct. 1903, pp. 821–23.
15. M. Aurel Stein, *Ancient Khotan*, 2 vols., Clarendon Press, Oxford, 1907, vol. II, pp. 548–56.
16. L. de la Vallée Poussin, *Théorie des douze causes*, Luzac, London, 1913.
17. N. Aiyaswami Sastri, *Ārya Śālistamba Sūtra*, Theosophical Society, Adyar, 1950.
18. *Mahāyāna-Sūtra-Saṁgraha*, P.L. Vaidya (ed.), Buddhist Sanskrit Texts series, vol. 17, Mithila Institute, Darbhanga, 1961.

Synopsis of Textual Sources

[Explained in last paragraph of Introduction]

Para.	*Av.*	*Bp.*	*Mp.*	*Ss.*	*Msl.*	*B.*	*C.*	*Pāli*	*SF*
1.	/						/	A2:29 M1:110	
2.	x						x	M1:110 M1:191 S3:120	
3.		xa					x	M1:263	/
4.		xa					/	M1:263	/
5.							/	D1:157	x
6.							/		/
7.		xab					x	U:80	x
8.		xb			x		x		/
9.	x					x	x	S2:25	/
10.		xb			x	x	x		
11.		xb			x	x	x		
12.		xb			x	/	x		
13.		xb			x	/	x		
14.		xb			x	/	x	S2:21 A1:173	x
15.		xb			x		x		
16.		xb			x		/		
17.		xb			x		/		
18.		xb			x		x		
19.		xb			x		/		
20.		xb			x		x		
21.			x			x	x		
22.			x	x	x	x	x	S2:10	
23.			x	x	x	x	x		/
24.			x	x	x	/	x	M1:421–3	/

Para.	*Av.*	*Bp.*	*Mp.*	*Ss.*	*Msl.*	*B.*	*C.*	*Pāli*	*SF*
25.			x	x	x	x	x		/
26.			x	x	x		x	M1:421	/
27.		xa	x	x	x	x	x	S2:3	/
28.		xa	x				x	S2:3	/
29.		xa	x	x	x		/	S2:3–4 S3:14	/
30.			x				/		/
31.			x				/		/
32.		xc	x	x	x			A1:223	x
33.		xc	x	x	x		x		x
34.		xc	x	x	x		x	M1:226	x
35.			x	x	x		x	M1:190	/
36.		xc	x	x	x		x		/
37.			x				x		/
38.		xc	x	x	x		x	M1:259	/
39.		xc	x	x	x		x		x
40.		xc	x	x	x		x		x
41.		xc	x	x	x		/		/
42.		xc	x	x	x		/		
43.		xc	x	x	x		/		
44.		xc	x	x	x		x		
45.			x	x	x		/	S2:112 S2:26	
46.			x				/	S2:88	
47.							x	S1:219	
48a.								M1:271	
48b.							x	D3:76	

Textual Symbols

In Sanskrit:

[ ] encloses Sanskrit recontructions from Tibetan for which there is no extant Sanskrit source.

( ) encloses extant Sanskrit material for which there is no Tibetan equivalent.

, indicates the half-slash with which some scribes punctuate Sanskrit.

| indicates the *Devanāgarī* punctuation slash.

Note: Textual sources for each paragraph are given in order of editorial preference at the beginning of each paragraph. Deviations from the preferred text are noted, except for minor variations in *sandhi*. Continuously written phrases are hyphenated where possible.

In English:

[ ] encloses material for which there is no Sanskrit source, but which exists in Tibetan translation.

( )* encloses material for which there is no Tibetan equivalent, but which exists in at least one Sanskrit source.

( ) encloses words not found in Sanskrit or Tibetan sources inserted to clarify the English translation.

In Tibetan:

Transcription follows Turrell Wylie, "A Standard System of Tibetan Transcription", *Harvard Journal of Asiatic Studies*, Vol. 22, pp. 261–67, 1959.

Abbreviations

A *Aṅguttara-nikāya*, PTS ed., with volume and page nos.
Asl. *Atthasālini*, PTS ed., with page no.
Av. *Abhidharmakoṣa-sphuṭārtha*, Yaṣomitra, Bauddha Bharati series, with chapter and verse nos.
B. *Bhāmatī*, Vācaspatimiṣra, Nyāyopādhyāya ed., Chowkhamba, Benares, 1935, with chapter and verse nos.
Bp. *Bodhicaryāvatāra-pañjikā*, Prajñākaramati, L. de la Vallée Poussin ed., with page no.
C. Chinese translation of the *Śālistamba-sūtra*, Taisho catalogue no. 709.
D *Dīgha-nikāya*, PTS ed., with volume and page nos.
DA *Dīgha-nikāya Atthakathā*, PTS ed., with volume and page no.
It. *Itivuttaka*, PTS ed., with verse no.
M *Majjhima-nikāya*, PTS ed., with volume and page nos.
Mp. *Madhyamakakārikā Prasannapadā*, Candrakīrti, L. de la Vallée Poussin ed., with page no.
Msl. *Mādhyamaka Śālistamba Sūtra*, V.V. Gokhale ed., in *Mahāyāna-sūtra-saṁgraha*, P.L. Vidya ed., with page no.
N. *Narthang* ed. of *Kanjur*.
NS Sastri, N. Aiyaswami, ed. of *Ārya Śālistamba Sūtra*, Adyar Library, 1950, Tibetan text with Sanskrit reconstruction.
P. Peking ed. of *Kanjur*.
Pt. *Paṭṭhāna*, PTS ed., with volume and page nos.
PTS Pali Text Society
S *Saṁyutta-nikāya*, PTS ed., with volume and page nos.
SBB Sacred Books of the Buddhists
SF Stein Fragment, fragments of a Tibetan Śālistamba *Sūtra*, ca. 750 A.D., printed in *Ancient Khotan*, M. Aurel Stein, Oxford, 1907.
Sn. *Sutta-nipāta*, PTS ed., with verse no.
Ss. *Śikṣāsamuccaya*, Śāntideva, Cecil Bendall ed., with page no.
T. Tibetan translation of the *Śālistamba Sūtra*, in Peking ed. of *Kanjur*.
TSs. Tibetan translation of the *Śikṣāsamuccaya* in Peking ed. of *Kanjur*, Vol. 102, pp. 240 (2–3) to 242 (2–8).
U. *Udāna*, PTS ed., with page no.
V. *Vinaya-piṭaka*, PTS ed., with volume and page nos.
Vbh. *Vibhaṅga*, PTS ed., with page no.
VP L. de la Vallee Poussin, *Théorie des douze causes*, Luzac, 1913, Tibetan text with Sanskrit reconstruction of the *Śālistamba Sūtra*.
Vsm. *Visuddhimagga*, Buddhaghosa, PTS ed., with page no.

The Śālistamba Sūtra

[In Sanskrit: *Ārya Śālistamba-nāma Mahāyāna Sūtra*. In Tibetan: *'phags pa sā lu'i ljang pa zhes bya ba theg pa chen po'i mdo*. Homage to all Buddhas and *Bodhisattvas*.]

||rgya gar skad du| ārya sha li stam ba na ma ma hā yā nā sū tra| bod skad du| 'phags pa sā lu'i ljang pa zhes bya ba theg pa chen po'i mdo|| sangs rgyas dang byang chub sems dpa' thams cad la phyag 'tshal lo||

1. Thus have I heard: [At one time,] the Lord was staying at Rājagṛha on Vulture Peak Mountain with a large company of monks, 1,250 monks, and many *Bodhisattvas,* [*Mahāsattvas.* At that time, the Venerable Śāriputra approached the place frequented[1] by Maitreya *Bodhisattva-mahāsattva.* When he approached, they exchanged many kinds of good and joyful words, and sat down together on a flat stone.][2]

Av. 3.28

1. Evaṁ mayā śrutam[3]| [ekasmin samaye] bhagavān rājagṛhe viharati gṛdhrakūṭe parvate mahatābhikṣusaṅghena sārdham-ardhatrayodaśabhir-bhikṣuśataiḥ sambahulaiś-ca bodhisattvair[4] [mahāsattvaiḥ| tasmin samaye āyuṣmān śāriputro yena maitreyabodhisattvamahāsattvasya gantavyaḥ pradeśas-tenopasamakramīd, upasaṁkramyānyo 'nyaṁ vividhasamyak saṁmodanīyāṁ kathāṁ vyatisārayitvā ubhau śilātale nyaṣīdatām||][5]

1. 'di skad bdag gis thos pa'i dus gcig na| bcom ldan 'das rgyal po'i khab na bya rgod phung po'i ri la dge slong stong nyis brgya lnga bcu'i dge slong gi dge 'dun chen po dang| byang chub sems dpa' sems dpa' chen po rab tu mang po dang thabs gcig tu bzhugs te| de'i tshe na tshe dang ldan pa shā ri'i bu byang chub sems dpa' sems dpa' chen po byams pa'i bgrod par bya ba'i sa phyogs ga la ba der song ste phyin nas phan tshun yang dag par dga' bar bya ba'i gtam rnam pa mang po byas nas 'dug ste| gnyis ka rdo leb la 'khod do||

(1) C: *caṅkramaḥ*, as NS. **(2)** C: Maitreya and Śāriputra sat together on a stone. **(3)** Av: °*mityādi.* **(4)** Av: °*riti.* **(5)** VP: *tena khalu punaḥ samayenāyuṣmān śāriputro yena maitreyasya bodhisattvasya mahāsattvasya parṣatsaṁnipātas tenopasamakramīd, upasaṁkramya parasparaṁ vividhasaṁmodanakathām upasaṁskṛtya samam ubhau śilātale nyaṣīdatām.* NS: *athāyuṣmān śāriputro yena maitreyabodhisattvasya mahāsattvasya caṅkramaḥ tenopasamakrāmīt| upasaṁkramya anyonyaṁ saṁmodanīyāṁ kathāṁ bahuvidhāṁ vyatisārayitvā ubhau śilātale upāviśatām||*

Pāli: *ekaṁ samayaṁ bhagavā rājagahe viharati gijjakūṭe pabbate. tena kho pana samayena sambahulā abhiññātā abhiññātā paribbājakā ... paṭivasanti* (A2:29, cp. V1:40) ... *atha kho te bhikkhū yenāyasmā mahākaccāno tenupasaṅkamiṁsu, upasaṅkamitvā āyasmatā mahākaccānena saddhiṁ sammodiṁsu, sammodanīyaṁ kathaṁ sārānīyaṁ vītisāretvā ekamantaṁ nisīdiṁsu* (M1:110).

2. [Then] the Venerable Śāriputra spoke thus to Maitreya *Bodhisattva* [*Mahāsattva*: "Maitreya, here, today, the Lord,] looking upon a stalk of rice, spoke this aphorism to the monks: 'Whoever, monks, sees conditioned arising sees Dharma, and whoever sees Dharma sees the Buddha.' Having said this the Lord became silent. What [Maitreya,] is the meaning of the aphorism spoken by the Lord? [1] What is conditioned arising? [2]What is Dharma? What is the Buddha?[2] How is it that seeing conditioned arising one sees Dharma? [How is it that seeing Dharma one sees the Buddha?]"

Av. 3.28
2. [atha] āyuṣmān śāriputro maitreyaṁ bodhisattvaṁ [mahāsattvam] etad avocat| [maitreya, adyātra bhagavatā] śālistambam-avalokya bhikṣubhyaḥ sūtram-idam-uktam yo bhikṣavaḥ pratītyasamutpādaṁ paśyati sa dharmaṁ paśyati, yo dharmaṁ paśyati sa buddhaṁ paśyati, ity-uktvā bhagavāṁs-tūṣṇīm-babhūva| tadasya [maitreya] bhagavatā[3] bhāṣitasya sūtrasya ko 'rthaḥ| pratītyasamutpādaḥ katamaḥ| dharmaḥ katamaḥ| buddhaḥ katamaḥ| kathaṁ ca pratītyasamutpādaṁ paśyan dharmaṁ paśyati[4]| [kathaṁ ca dharmaṁ paśyan buddhaṁ paśyati||]

2. de nas tshe dang ldan pa shā ri'i bus byang chub sems dpa' sems dpa' chen po byams pa la 'di skad ces smras so|| byams pa deng 'dir bcom ldan 'das kyis sā lu'i ljang pa la gzigs nas dge slong rnams la mdo 'di gsungs so|| dge slong dag sus rten cing 'brel bar 'byung ba mthong ba des chos mthong ngo|| sus chos mthong ba des sangs rgyas mthong ngo zhes de skad bka' stsal nas| bcom ldan 'das cang mi gsung bar gyur na byams pa bde bar gshegs pas bka' stsal pa'i mdo sde'i don ni ci| [5] rten cing 'brel bar 'byung ba ni gang| chos ni gang| sangs rgyas ni gang| ji ltar rten cing 'brel bar 'byung ba mthong na chos mthong| ji ltar chos mthong na sang rgyas mthong|

(1) C. inserts: What is the meaning of the statement: "Whoever sees ... sees the Buddha?" In all, what is the meaning of speaking like this? **(2-2)** C. omits. **(3)** T: *sugatena.* **(4)** Av: °*tītyādi*, omitting last sentence and paras. 3-8. **(5)** P. inserts: *dge slong dag sus.*

Pāli: *ekamantaṁ nisinnā kho te bhikkhū āyasmantaṁ mahākaccānam etadavocuṁ idaṁ kho no āvuso kaccāna bhagavā saṅkhittena uddesaṁ uddisitvā vitthārenaatthaṁ avibhajitvā uṭṭhayāsanā vihāraṁ paviṭṭho* (M1:110) ... *yo paṭiccasamuppādaṁ passati so dhammaṁ passati, yo dhammaṁ passati so paṭiccasamuppādaṁ passatīti* (M1:191). ... *yo kho vikkali dhammaṁ passati so maṁ passati, yo maṁ passati so dhammaṁ passati* (S3:120).

3. [1]When this was said, Maitreya *Bodhisattva-mahāsattva* spoke thus to the Venerable Śāriputra: [Reverend Śāriputra,] regarding what was said by the Lord, the master of Dharma, the omniscient:[1] "He monks, who sees conditioned arising, sees Dharma, and he who sees Dharma, sees the Buddha." Therein, what is conditioned arising? [The phrase "conditioned arising" means: this being, that occurs; from the arising of this, that arises.][2] That is to say: ignorance conditions (mental) formations. (Mental) formations condition consciousness. Consciousness conditions name-and-form. Name-and-form conditions the six (sense) entrances. The six entrances condition contact. Contact conditions sensation. Sensation conditions desire. Desire conditions grasping. Grasping conditions becoming. Becoming conditions birth. Birth conditions decay and death, and grief, lamentation, suffering, depression and anxiety [arise. [3]Thus the arising of this entire great mass of suffering occurs.][3]

Bp. 386
3. evam-ukte maitreyo bodhisattvo mahāsattva āyuṣmantaṁ śāriputram[4]-etad-avocat [bhadanta śāriputra] yad-uktaṁ bhagavatā dharmasvāminā sarvajñena, yo bhikṣavaḥ pratītyasamutpādaṁ paśyati sa dharmaṁ paśyati| yo dharmaṁ paśyati sa buddhaṁ paśyati| tatra katamaḥ pratītyasamutpādo nāma, [pratītyasamutpādo nāma yaduta asmin satīdam bhavati, asyotpādād idam-utpadyate|][5] yadidam-avidyāpratyayāḥ saṁskārāḥ, saṁskārapratyayaṁ vijñānaṁ, vijñānapratyayaṁ nāmarūpaṁ, nāmarūpapratyayaṁ ṣaḍāyatanaṁ, ṣaḍāyatanapratyayaḥ sparśaḥ| sparśapratyayā vedanā, vedanāpratyayā tṛṣṇā, tṛṣṇāpratyayam-upādānaṁ, upādānapratyayo bhavaḥ, bhavapratyayā jātiḥ, jātipratyayā jarāmaraṇaśokaparidevaduḥkhadaurmanasyopāyāsā[6] [bhavanti| evam-asya kevalasya mahato duḥkhaskandhasya samudayo bhavati||]

3. de skad ces smras pa dang|byang chub sems dpa' sems dpa' chen po byams pas tshe dang ldan pa śā ra dva ti'i bu la 'di skad ces smras so|| btsun pa shā ri'i bu 'di la bcom ldan 'das kyi chos kyi bdag po tham cad mkhyen pas dge slong dag sus rten cing 'brel bar 'byung ba mthong ba des chos mthong ngo| sus chos mthong ba des sangs rgyas mthong ngo zhes gsungs pa de la rten cing 'brel bar 'byung ba gang zhe na| rten cing 'brel bar 'byung ba zhes bya ba ni 'di lta ste| 'di yod pas 'di 'byung la 'di skyes pa'i phyir 'di skye ba ste| gang 'di ma rig pa'i rkyen gyis 'du byed rnams| 'du byed kyi rkyen gyis rnam par shes pa| rnam par shes pa'i rkyen gyis ming dang gzugs| ming dang gzugs kyi rkyen gyis skye mched drug| skye mched drug gi rkyen gyis reg pa| reg pa'i rkyen gyis tshor ba| tshor ba'i rkyen gyis sred pa| sred pa'i rkyen gyis len pa| len pa'i rkyen gyis srid pa| srid pa'i rkyen gyis skye ba| skye ba'i rkyen gyis rga shi dang| mya ngan dang smre sngags 'don pa dang| sdug bsngal ba dang| yid mi bde ba dang| 'khrug pa rnams 'byung ste| de ltar sdug bsngal gyi phung po chen po 'ba' zhig po 'di 'byung bar 'gyur ro|

(1-1) C: At that time Maitreya said to Śāriputra, "The Buddha, the Lord often says: ...". **(2)** This phrase, omitted in C., and included only in T., refers to the specific relationship of a giveṅ cause to its effect, i.e., "This being, that (and not another) occurs". Cp. para. 9: *idaṁ pratyayatā phalam.* VP: see Bp. ix, 73, 474; Mp. 9, *Mahāvastu* ii, 285; S2:65; M2:32; M3:63; U:1. **(3-3)** C: The coming together of many sufferings is the cause of the great mass of suffering. **(4)** T: *śāradvati-putram.* **(5)** Cp. M1:263 etc. **(6)** Bp: °*opāyāsāḥ*, omitting para. 4 down to *nirudhyante.*

Pāli: (When asked to elucidate the Buddha's words, as in Pāli for Para. 2, head disciples customarily praise the Buddha, often suggesting that the questioner should have asked the Buddha himself:) *so hāvuso bhagavā jānaṁ jānāti passaṁ passati, cakkubhūto ñānabhūto dhammabhūto brahmabhūto, vattā pavattā, atthassa ninnetā amatassa dātā, dhammassāmī tathāgato* (M1:111) ... *imasmiṁ sati idaṁ hoti, imassuppādā idaṁ uppajjati yadidaṁ avijjāpaccayā sankhārā ... jātipaccayā jarāmaraṇaṁ sokaparidevadukkhadomanassupāyāsā sambhavanti, evametassa kevalassa dukkhakkhandhassa samudayo hoti* (M1:262-3, etc.).

SF: ... *rky(e)nd kyis reg pa| reg pa'i rkyend kyis tshor ba'| tshor ba'i rkyend kyis sred pa| sred pa'i rkyend kyis lend pa| ... sdug bsngal ba dang| yi mug pa dang| 'khrug pa rnams 'byung ste| de ltar sdug bsngal gyi phung po chen po 'di 'b(yung)* ....

4. [Similarly, from the cessation of ignorance there is the cessation of (mental) formations. From the cessation of (mental) formations there is the cessation of consciousness. From the cessation of conscoiusness there is the cessation of name-and-form. From the cessation of name-and-form there is the cessation of the six (sense) entrances. From the cessation of the six (sense) entrances there is the cessation of contact. From the cessation of contact there is the cessation of sensation. From the cessation of sensation there is the cessation of desire. From the cessation of desire there is the cessation of grasping. From the cessation of grasping there is the cessation of becoming. from the cessation of becoming there is the cessation of birth. From the cessation of birth, decay and death, grief, lamentation, suffering, depression and anxiety] cease. Thus is the cessation of this entire great mass of suffering. This is called "conditioned arising" [by the Lord].

Bp. 387

4. [tatrāvidyānirodhat saṁskāranirodhaḥ, saṁskāranirodhād vijñānanirodho, vijñānanirodhān nāmarūpanirodho, nāmarūpanirodhāt ṣaḍāyatananirodhaḥ ṣaḍāyatananirodhāt sparśanirodhaḥ, sparśanirodhād vedanānirodho, vedanānirodhāt tṛṣṇānirodhas, tṛṣṇānirodhād upādānanirodha, upādānanirodhād bhavanirodho, bhavanirodhāj jātinirodho, jātinirodhāj jarāmaranaśokaparideva duḥkhadaurmanasyopāyāsā] nirudhyante| evam-asya kevalasya mahato duḥkhaskandhasya nirodho bhavati| ayam-ucyate pratītyasamutpāda [bhagavatā]||

4. de la ma rig pa 'gags pas 'du byed 'gag| 'du byed 'gags pas rnam par shes pa 'gag| rnam par shes pa 'gags pas ming dang gzugs 'gag| ming dang gzugs 'gags pas skye mched drug 'gag| skye mched drug 'gags pas reg pa 'gag| reg pa 'gags pas tshor ba 'gag| tshor ba 'gags pas sred pa 'gag| sred pa 'gags pas len pa 'gag| len pa 'gags pas srid pa 'gag| srid pa 'gags pas skye ba 'gag| skye ba 'gags pas rga shi dang| mya ngan dang| smre sngags 'don pa dang sdug bsngal dang| yid me bde ba dang| 'khrug pa rnams 'gag par 'gyur te| de ltar sdug bsngal gyi phung po chen po 'ba' zhig po 'di 'gag par 'gyur ro| 'di nas bcom ldan 'das kyis rten cing 'brel bar 'byung ba zhes gsungs so||

(1) Bp. is oddly incomplete for para. 4; C. has last sentence only. **(2)** Bp. omits paras. 5-6.

Pāli: *avijjāya tveva asesavirāganirodhā saṅkhāranirodho, saṅkhāranirodhā viññāṇanirodho ... sokaparideva dukkhadomanass upāyāsā nirujjhanti, evam etassa kevalassa dukkhakkhandhassa nirodho hoti* (M1:263, etc.).

SF: *...'gag| rnam par shes pa 'gags pas mying dang gzugs 'gag| mying dang gzugs 'gags pas ... tshor ba 'gags pas sred pa 'gag| sred pa 'gags pas lend pa 'gag| lend pa 'gags pas srid pa 'gags ... bsngal ba dang| yi mug pa dang 'khrug pa rnams 'gags par 'gyur te| de ltar sdug bsngal gyi phung po chen (p)o ... zhes gsungs so||*

5. [What is Dharma? It is the Noble Eight-fold Path, namely: right view, right thought, right speech, right action, right livelihood, right effort, right mindfulness, and right concentration. This Noble Eight-fold Path, the attainment of (its) fruit(s) and Nirvana rolled into one is called Dharma by the Lord.][1]

T. only

5. [dharmaḥ katamaḥ| āryāṣṭāṅgamārgas-tadyathā samyag-dṛṣṭiḥ samyak-saṁkalpaḥ samyag-vāk samyak-karmāntaḥ, samyag-ājīvaḥ samyag-vyāyāmaḥ samyak-smṛtiḥ samyak-samādhiś-ca| [2]ayam-āryāṣṭāṅgamārgaḥ iti phalaprāptiś-ca nirvāṇaṁ-ca aikadhyam-abhisaṁkṣipya dharma ity-ucyate bhagavatā|[2]]

5. chos gang zhe na| 'phags pa'i lam yan lag brgyad pa ste| 'di lta ste| yang dag pa'i lta ba dang| yang dag pa'i rtog pa dang| yang dag pa'i ngag dang| yang dag pa'i las kyi mtha' dang| yang dag pa'i 'tsho ba dang| yang dag pa'i rtsol ba dang| yang dag pa'i dran pa dang| yang dag pa'i ting nge 'dzin to| 'di ni 'phags pa'i lam yan lag brgyad pa zhes bya ste| 'bras bu thob pa dang| mya ngan las 'das pa gcig tu bsdus te| bcom ldan 'das kyis chos so zhes bka' stsal to||

(1) For para. 5, C: What is Dharma? (It is) the Noble Eight-fold Path (which is) divided into attaining Nirvana and fruits. (Thus) the Tathāgata briefly explains Dharma. (2-2) VP: *imam-āryāṣṭaṅgamārgam iti phalaprāptim ca nirvāṇam aikadhyam abhisaṁkṣipya dharma ity ucyate.* NS: ...*ayamukto bhagavatā āryāṣṭāṅgiko mārgaḥ phalalābhanirvāṇaikasaṁgṛhīto dharmaḥ.*

Pāli: *katamo pana bhante maggo, katamo paṭipadā, etesaṁ dhammānaṁ saccikiriyāyāti. ayaṁ eva ariyo aṭṭhaṅgiko maggo seyyathīdaṁ sammādiṭṭhi sammāsaṁkappo sammāvācā sammākammanto sammā ājivo sammāvāyāmo sammāsati sammāsamādhi* (D1:157, etc.).

SF: *chos gang zhe na'| 'phags pa'i lam yan lag brgyad pa ste| 'di' lta ste yang dag pa'i lta ba dang| yang dag pa'i rtog pa dang| yang dag pa'i ngag ... 'tsho ba dang| yang dag pa'i rtsol ba dang| yang dag pa'i dran ba dang| yang dag pa'i tinge 'dzind to| 'di ni 'phags pa'i lam yan lag brgyad pa zhes bya ste 'bras bu rnyed pa ... te bcom ldan 'das kyis chos so zhes bka stsald to||*

6. [What, then is the Buddha, the Lord? He who, because he comprehends all *dharmas*,[1] is called the Buddha, is endowed with the wisdom-eye[2] and the Dharma-body[3]. He sees the *dharmas*[4] of both the learner and the learned.][5]

T. only
6. [tatra buddho bhagavān katamaḥ| yaḥ sarvadharmāvabodhād buddha ity-ucyate, sa āryaprajñācakśuś-ca dharmaśarrīraṁś-ca[6] sampannaḥ| śaikṣāśaikṣāṁś-ca dharmān paśyati||][7]

6. de la sangs rgyas bcom ldan 'das gang zhe na| sus chos thams chad thugs su chud pa'i phyir sangs rgyas shes bya ste| des 'phags pa'i shes rab kyi spyan dang chos kyi sku dang ldan pa dang| slob pa dang mi slob pa'i chos de dag gzigs pa'o||

(1) Here, *dharma* = "things" or "laws, principles". (2) Cp. M1:293; D3:219; It:52. (3) N.B. *dharmaśarīra* in para. 7; probably the same here. (4) Here, *dharma* = "rules, practices". "Learner" = *śaikṣa*, one who must undergo training. "Learned" = *aśaikṣa*, an *arahat* or perfected one, who no longer needs training. Cp. M3:76, D3:218-19. (5) For para. 6, C: What is the Buddha? He can realize all *dharmas*; therefore he is called the Buddha. If, with the wisdom-eye, one sees the true Dharma-body, one can achieve *bodhi* (and) the *dharma* of the learner. (6) See Bp. verification of *śarīra* in para. 7. below. (7) VP: *tatra katamo buddho bhagavān? yaḥ sarvadharmāvabodhād buddha iti sa āryaprañācakṣur dharmakāyasampannaḥ śaikṣān aśaikṣāṁś ca dharmān paśyati. NS: tatra katamo buddho bhagavān| yaḥ sarvadharmāvabodhādbuddha ucyate sa āryaprajñānetraḥ dharmakāyasamanvitaḥ śaikṣāśaikṣadharmānimān paśyati|*

SF: *de la sangs rgyas bcom ldan 'das gang zhe na| sus chos thams cad thugsu chud pa'i phyir sangs rgyas zhe(s) ... chos kyi skus byang chub byed pa dang| slob pa dang mi slob pa'i chos rnams gzigs so||*

7. How, then, does one see conditioned arising? In this connection, it is said by the Lord: "Whoever sees this conditioned arising (which is), always and ever devoid of soul, truly undistorted, without soul,[1] unborn, not become, not made, not compounded,[2] unobstructed, inconceivable,[3] glorious, fearless, ungraspable, inexhaustible and by nature[4] never stilled, (he sees Dharma). And whoever sees Dharma (which is) also always and ever devoid of soul ... and by nature never stilled, he sees the unsurpassable Dharma-body,[5] the Buddha, by exertion based on right knowledge in clear understanding[6] of the noble Dharma."[7]

Bp. 576 Bp. 387
7. [8]tatra kathaṁ pratītyasamutpādaṁ paśyati| ihoktaṁ bhagavatā,[8] ya imaṁ pratītyasamutpādaṁ satatasamitaṁ nirjīvaṁ yathāvad-aviparītam-ajīvam[9]-ajātam-abhūtam-akṛtam[10]-asaṁskṛtam-apratigham-anālambanaṁ śivam-abhayam-anāhāryam-avyayam-avyupaśamasvabhāvaṁ[11] paśyati, (sa dharmaṁ paśyati| yastu)[12] evaṁ satatasamitaṁ [13]nirjīvam-ity-ādi pūrvat,[13] yāvad-avyupaśamasvabhāvaṁ [14] paśyati, so'nuttaradharmaśarīraṁ buddhaṁ paśyati| āryadharmābhisamaye samyag-jñānād-upanayenaiva.||[15]

7. de la rten cing 'brel bar 'byung ba mthong ba ji lta bu zhe na| 'di la bcom ldan 'das kyis sus rten cing 'brel bar 'byung ba rtag pa dang| srog med pa dang| srog dang bral ba dang| ji lta bu nyid dang| ma nor ba dang| ma skyes pa dang| ma byung ba dang| ma byas pa dang| 'dus ma byas pa dang| thogs pa med pa dang| dmigs pa med pa dang| zhi ba dang| 'jigs pa med pa dang| mi 'phrogs pa dang| rnam par zhi ba ma yin pa'i rang bzhin du mthong ba ste| gang gis tshul 'dhi 'dra bar chos la'ang rtag pa| srog med pa dang| srog dang bral ba dang| ji lta bu nyid dang| ma nor ba dang| ma skyes pa dang| ma byung ba dang| ma byas pa dang| 'dus ma byas pa dang| thog pa med pa dang| dmigs pa med pa dang| zhi ba dang| 'jigs pa med pa dang| mi 'phrogs pa dang| rnam par zhi ba ma yin pa'i rang bzhin du mthong ba de 'phags pa'i chos mngon par rtogs te| yang dag pa'i ye shes dang ldan pas bla na med pa'i chos kyi skur sangs rgyas mthong ngo zhes gsungs so||

(1) *nirjīvam ... ajīvam*: Buddhaghosa uses a similar Pāli phrase in several definitions of Dhamma: Asl.38; DA1:22, 99. (2) Cp. U:80, which, however, deals with Nirvana. (3) *Anālambana* = Pāli *anārammaṇa* = lit. "without base", but in this instance a technical term meaning "without a basis for sense perception", so here the term probably means "without an objective sensual basis" i.e. "inconceivable". (4) *Svabhāva* = lit. "self-existence", but here simply "nature" as in "good-natured". See *svabhāva* in para. 32. (5) *Dharma-śarīra* (T: *chos kyi sku*). The odd Sanskrit term, where *Dharma-kāya* would be expected, is confirmed by Bp. 387 and 576. Cp. para. 6. (6) *Abhisamaya* (T: *mngon par rtogs*), perfect and absolutely clear understanding developed through initial hearing (*śruta*), study (*cinta*) and meditation (*bhavanā*), ultimately equivalent to enlightenment. (7) For para. 7, C: How is it that seeing conditioned arising is seeing Dharma, and seeing Dharma is seeing Buddha? The Buddha makes this statement: "Conditioned arising is eternal, continuously arising without soul. Seen as it really is (it is) undistorted, without soul, not made, not having action, unceasing, not active (*wu wei*), without mental basis, quiescent and signless. For this reason, seeing

conditioned arising is seeing Dharma, (which is) eternal, continuously arising. ... For this reason, seeing conditioned arising is seeing the unsurpassable path and the complete *Dharma-kāya*. **(8-8)** Bp. 387 omits. **(9)** Bp. 387 omits *ajīvam*; T. puts before *nirjīvam*. **(10)** Bp. 387 omits *akṛtam*. **(11)** Bp. 387 and T: °*abhayam-ahāryam-avyupaśama*°. **(12)** T. omits. **(13-13)** Bp. 387 omits. T. has ellipsis but repeats entire formula. **(14)** Bp. 387 inserts *dharmaṁ*. **(15)** Bp. 387 omits sentence with ellipsis *peyālaṁ*, resuming citation with para. 27.

Pāli (referring to nirvana): *atthi bhikkhave ... appatiṭṭhaṁ appavattaṁ anāramaṇam ... ajātaṁ abhūtaṁ akataṁ asankhataṁ* (U:80).

SF: *de la ji ltar na rtend cing 'breld par 'byung ba mthong zhe na| 'di la bcom ldan '(das) ... dang srog myed pa dang srog dang bral ba dang ji lta bu nyid dang ma nord pa dang ma skyes pa dang ma byung ba dang ma byas pa dang thogs pa myed pa dang dmyigs pa myed pa dang zhi ba dang myi 'gigs pa dang ... dang ma nord pa dang ma skyes pa dang ma byung ba dang ma byas pa dang 'dus ma byas pa dang thogs pa myed pa dang dmyigs pa myed pa dang zhi ... (rt)ogs shin yang dag pa'i ye shes thob pas bla na myed pa'i chos kyi skur sangs rgyas mthong ngo zhes gsungs so||*

8. Why is it called conditioned arising? It is causal and conditional, not non-causal and non-conditional, [Therefore it is called conditioned arising.][1]

Bp. 577 Msl. 108

8. pratītyasamutpāda iti kasmād-ucyate| sahetukaḥ sapratyayo nāhetuko nāpratyaya[s tasmāt pratītyasamutpāda] ity-ucyate|[2]

8. smras pa| ci'i phyir rten cing 'brel bar 'byung ba zhes bya| smras pa| rgyu dang bcas rkyen dang bcas pa la bya'i| rgyu med rkyen med pa la ni ma yin te| de'i phyir rten cing 'brel bar 'byung ba zhes bya'o||

(1) For para. 8, C: Venerable Śāriputra asked Maitreya, "Why is it called conditioned arising?" Maitreya answered: "It has causes and conditions, therefore it is called the *dharma* of conditioned arising." **(2)** Bp. adds *peyālaṁ*, omitting para. 9.

SF: *smras pa' (ci'i phyir) ... (rkyen)d myed pa la ma yin te| de'i phyir rtend cing 'breld par 'byung ba zhes bya'o||*

9. [In this connection, the characteristics of conditioned arising are given in brief by the Lord:] "Results (come about by) specific conditionality.[1] Whether or not Tathāgatas arise, constant is this Dharma-nature, the constancy of Dharma, the law of Dharma, suchness, true suchness, changeless suchness, actuality, truth, (reality,)* undistorted and immutable."[2]

Av. 3.28 B. 2.19

9. [3][tatra pratītyasamutpādalakṣaṇaṁ saṁkṣiptoktaṁ bhagavatā,] idaṁ pratyayaphalam|[3] utpādād-vā tathāgatānām-anutpādād-vā (tathāgatānāṁ)[4] sthitaiveyam[5] [6] dharmatā dharmasthititā dharmaniyāmatā[7] [8] [9]tathatā avitathatā ananyatathatā bhūtatā satyatā (tattvam) aviparītatā 'viparyastateti[9]|

9. de la bcom ldan 'das kyis rten cing 'brel bar 'byung ba'i mtshan nyid mdor bka' stsal pa| rkyen 'di nyid kyi 'bras bu ste| de bzhin gshegs pa rnams byung yang rung ma byung yang rung| chos rnams kyi chos nyid 'di ni 'dug pa'o zhes bya ba nas gang 'di chos nyid dang| chos gnas pa nyid dang| chos mi 'gyur ba nyid dang| rten cing 'brel bar 'byung ba mthun pa dang| de bzhin nyid dang| ma nor ba de bzhin nyid dang| gzhan ma yin pa de bzhin nyid dang| yang dag pa nyid dang| bden pa kho na dang| ma nor ba nyid dang| phyin ci ma log pa nyid ces bya ba'i bar du gsungs so||

(1) Cp. Pali *idappaccayatā* (S2:25, A1:286) which according to Buddhaghosa refers to the specific relation of the causes to the effects in the *paṭiccasamuppāda* formula, or to the relation of specific causes to specific effects in general. (Vsm. 518; cp. S1:136); C: As T., but: "Through this cause, that result can arise". **(2)** For last sentence, C: (If) *Tathāgatas* appear in the world, there is the *dharma* of conditioned arising. (If) *Tathāgatas* do not appear in the world, still there is the *dharma* of conditioned arising. Its nature is constant, without any disturbance, actual suchness, not non-suchness. This is the true, actual Dharma, the undistorted Dharma. **(3-3)** Av. omits. B: *pratītyasamutpādalakṣaṇam-uktaṁ buddhena idaṁ pratyayaphalam-iti.* **(4)** T. and B. omit. **(5)** B: *°vaiṣā.* **(6)** T. inserts *dharmāṇam.* **(7)** T: *dharmābhavatā.* **(8)** T. and B. insert *pratītyasamutpādānulomatā.* **(9-9)** B. omits. Av: *°tety-evam-ādi bhagavān maitreyavacanam|.*

Pāli: *uppādā vā tathāgatānaṁ anuppāda vā tathāgatānaṁ ṭhitā va sā dhātu dhammaṭṭhitatā dhammaniyāmatā idappaccayatā ... yā tatra tathatā avitathatā anaññathatā idappaccayatā. ayaṁ vuccati, bhikkhave, paṭiccasamuppādo* (S2:25-6).

SF: *de la bcom ldan 'das kyis rtend cing 'brel par ... (ya)ng rung ma byung yang rung chos rnams kyi chos nyid 'di ni 'dug pa'o zhes bya ba nas| gang 'di chos nyid dang chos gnas pa nyid dang ... (de bzhin nyid da)ng| gzhan ma yin ba de bzhin nyid dang| yang dag pa nyid dang bden ba kho na dang| de kho na nyid dang ma nord pa nyid dang phyin ci ma ...*

10. Furthermore, this conditioned arising arises from two (principles)*. From what two (principles does it arise)*? From a causal relation and a conditional relation.[1] Moreover, it should be seen as two-fold: objective and subjective.

Bp. 577 Msl. 108 B. 2.19

10. atha ca[2] punar-ayaṁ pratītyasamutpādo dvābhyāṁ (kāraṇābhyām)[3] utpadyate[4]| katamābhyāṁ dvābhyāṁ (kāraṇābhyām utpadyate)[5]| [6] hetūpanibandhataḥ pratyayopanibandhataś-ca[7]| so'pi dvividho draṣṭavyaḥ, bāhyaś-cādhyātmikaś-ca|[8]

10. 'di ltar yang rten cing 'brel bar 'byung ba 'di gnyis kyi phyir 'byung ste| gnyis gang zhe na| 'di lta ste| rgyu dang 'brel ba dang| rkyen dang 'brel ba'i phyir ro|| de yang phyi'i dang| nang gi dang| rnam pa gnyis su blta'o||

(1) C: The first is cause. The second is result. (!) (2) B. omits. (3) Bp., Msl. omit. (4) B: *bhavati.* (5) B. omits. (6) T. inserts: *yadidam.* (7) Msl: *ceti.* (8) B: *sa punar-dvividhaḥ bāhya ādhyātmikaś-ca.*

11. What, then, is the causal relation in objective conditioned arising?[1] It is as when a sprout comes from a seed, from the sprout a leaf, from the leaf a shoot, from the shoot a stalk, from the stalk (a swelling, from the swelling)* a bud, from the bud (a calyx, from the calyx)* a flower, and from the flower a fruit. When there is no seed, a sprout does not occur, and so on until: when there is no flower, a fruit does not occur.[2] But when there is a seed, the development of a sprout occurs, and so on until: when there is a flower, the development of a fruit occurs. It does not occur to the seed, "I cause the sprout to develop." Nor does it occur to the sprout, "I am developed by the seed", and so on until: it does not occur to the flower, "I cause the fruit to develop". Nor does it occur to the fruit, "I am developed by the flower". [3]But still, when there is a seed, the development, the manifestation of the sprout occurs, and so on until: when there is a flower, the development, the manifestation of the fruit occurs. Thus is the causal relation in objective conditioned arising to be seen.[3]

Bp. 577 Msl. 108 B. 2.19

11. tatra bāhyasya pratītyasamutpādasya hetūpanibandhaḥ katamaḥ[4]| yadidaṁ bījād-aṅkuraḥ, aṅkurāt-pattraṁ, pattrāt-kāṇḍaṁ, kāṇḍān-nālaṁ, nālād-(gaṇḍaḥ, gaṇḍād)[5] garbhaṁ, garbāc-(chūkaḥ| śūkāt) puṣpam| puṣpāt-phalam-iti| asati bīje'ṅkuro na bhavati, yāvad-asati puṣpe phalam na bhavati| sati tu bije'ṅkurasyābhinirvṛttir-bhavati, evaṁ yāvat-sati puṣpe phalasyābhinirvṛttir-bhavati||[6] tatra [7] bījasya naivaṁ bhavati, aham-aṅkuram-abhinirvartayāmīti[8]| [9]aṅkurasyāpi naivaṁ bhavati, aham-bījenābhinirvartita[10] iti| evaṁ yāvat-puṣpasya naivaṁ bhavati, ahaṁ phalam-abhinirvartayāmīti[11]| [12] phalasyāpi naivaṁ bhavati, ahaṁ puṣpenābhinirvartitamiti[13]| [14]atha punar-bīje[15] sati [16] aṅkurasyābhinirvṛttir-bhavati, prādurbhāvaḥ[17]| evaṁ yāvat-puṣpe sati phalasyābhinirvṛttir-bhavati, prādurbhāvaḥ[18]| evaṁ [19] bāhyasya pratītyasamutpādasya hetūpanibandho draṣṭavyaḥ||[14]

11. de la phyi rol gyi rten cing 'brel bar 'byung ba rgyu dang 'brel ba gang zhe na| 'di lta ste| sa bon las myu gu| myu gu las 'dab ma| 'dab ma las sdong bu| sdong bu las sbu bu| sbu bu las snying po| snying po las me tog| me tog las 'bras bu'o|| sa bon med na myu gu mi 'byung ste| me tog med na 'bras bu'i bar du yang mi 'byung ngo|| sa bon yod na myu gu mngon par 'grub par 'gyur te| de bzhin du me tog yod na 'bras bu'i bar du mngon par 'grub par 'gyur ro|| de la sa bon ni 'di snyam du bdag gis myu gu mngon par bsgrub bo snyam du mi sems so|| myu gu yang 'di snyam du bdag ni sa bon gyis mngon par bsgrubs so snyam du mi sems so|| de bzhin du me tog kyang 'di snyam du bdag gis 'bras bu mngon par bsgrub bo

snyam du mi sems pa'i bar du ste|| 'bras bu yang 'di snyam du bdag ni me tog gis mngon par bsgrubs so snyam du mi sems mod kyi| 'on kyang sa bon yod na myu gu mngon par 'grub cing 'byung bar 'gyur ba nas de bzhin du me tog yod na 'bras bu'i bar du yang mngon par 'grub cing 'byung bar 'gyur te| de ltar phyi rol gyi rtẹn cing 'brel bar 'byung ba rgyu dang 'brel bar blta'o||

(1) C: "Objective conditioned arising arises from what?" (omitting two of the following ten stages, *gaṇḍha* and *śūka*, as does T., probably because of insufficient botanical vocabulary, but note B. omits *gaṇḍha*). **(2)** C: ... until: there is no flower or fruit. **(3-3)** C: But in fact the seed can produce the sprout. Thus it is called objective causal arising. **(4)** B. omits. **(5)** B. and T. omit. **(6)** B: °*bije'ṅkuro bhavati yāvat puṣpe sati phalam iti.* **(7)** Msl. inserts: *ca punar.* **(8)** Msl. omits *abhi-*. B: ... *bhavati jñānam-aham-aṅkuraṁ nirvartayāmīti.* **(9)** Msl. inserts: *etena nirhatvam.* **(10)** B: *jñānam ahaṁ bījena nirvartita iti.* **(11)** B. omits *abhi-*. **(12)** B. inserts *evaṁ.* **(13)** Bp: *bījenābhi*° **(14-14)** B: *tasmād-asaty-api caitanye bījādīnām-asaty-api cānyasminnadhiṣṭhātari kārya-kāraṇabhāvaniyamo dṛśyate| ukto hetūpanibandhaḥ.* **(15)** Msl. omits *punar.* **(16)** Msl. inserts *ca.* **(17)** Msl: °*abhinirvṛttiḥ prādurbhāvo bhavati.* **(18)** Ditto. **(19)** Msl. inserts *ca.*

12. How is the conditional relation in objective conditioned arising to be seen? As the coming together of six factors. As the coming together of what six factors? Namely, as the coming together of the earth, water, heat, wind, space and season factors[1] is the conditional relation in objective conditioned arising to be seen.[2]

Bp. 578 Msl. 109 B. 2.19

12. [3] kathaṁ bāhyasya pratītyasamutpādasya pratyayopanibandho draṣṭavyaḥ| ṣaṇṇāṁ dhātūnāṁ samavāyāt| [4] katameṣāṁ ṣaṇṇāṁ dhātūnāṁ samavāyāt| yadidaṁ pṛthivyaptejovāyvākāśartusamavāyāt,[5] bāhyasya pratītyasamutpādasya pratyayopanibandho[6] draṣṭavyaḥ|[7]

12. phyi rol gyi rten cing 'brel bar 'byung ba rkyen dang 'brel ba ji ltar blta zhe na| khams drug 'dus pa'i phyir te| khams drug po gang dag 'dus pa'i phyir zhe na| 'di lta ste| sa dang| chu dang| me dang| rlung dang| nam mkha' dang| dus kyi khams rnams 'dus pa las phyi rol gyi rten cing 'brel bar 'byung ba rkyen dang 'brel bar blta'o||

(1) Season (*ṛtu*) is not technically a factor (*dhātu*), but here substitutes for consciousness (*vijñāna*, cp. para. 23) for the sake of formal balance. Here, Bp. omits *dhātu*, and Msl. omits *ṛtu*, both thereby avoiding a technical mistake. T. includes both terms. C. omits "factors" to end of para. 12, see n. 2. **(2)** For para. 12, C: What is called external conditioned arising? That which is called earth ... season. **(3)** Msl. inserts *punaḥ*. **(4)** Msl. inserts: *svabhāvadharaṇād-dhātuḥ.* **(5)** Msl: °*ākaśadhātusamavayād.* **(6)** Bp.omits *upa-*. **(7)** B. glosses para. 12.

13. Therein, the earth-factor performs the function of supporting the seed. The water-factor waters the seed. The heat-factor matures[1] the seed. The wind-factor brings out[2] the seed. The space-factor performs the function of not obstructing[3] the seed. [4]Season[5] performs the function of transforming the seed. Without these conditions, the development of the sprout from the seed does not occur. But when the objective earth-factor is not deficient, and likewise the water, heat, wind, space and season factors are not deficient, then from the coming together of all these, when the seed is ceasing the development of the sprout occurs.[4]

Bp. 578 Msl. 109 B 2.19
13. tatra pṛthivīdhātur-bījasya saṁdhāraṇakṛtyaṁ[6] karoti| [7]abdhātur-bījaṁ snehayati| tejodhātur-bījaṁ parīpācayati| vāyudhātur-bījam-abhinirharati| [8] ākāśadhātur-bījasyānāvaraṇakṛtyaṁ karoti| ṛtur-api bījasya pariṇāmanākṛtyaṁ[9] karoti| [10]asatsveṣu[11] pratyayeṣu bījād-aṅkurasyābhinirvṛttir[12] na bhavati| yadā bāhyaś-ca pṛthivīdhātur-avikalo bhavati, evam-aptejovāyvākāśaṛtudhātavaś-cāvikalā bhavanti, tataḥ[13] sarveṣāṁ samavāyāt, bīje nirudhyamāne 'ṅkurasyābhinirvṛttir-bhavati||[10]

13. de la sa'i khams ni sa bon rten pa'i bya ba byed do|| chu'i khams ni sa bon brlan pa'i bya ba byed do|| me'i khams ni sa bon yongs su dro ba'i bya ba byed do|| rlung gi khams ni sa bon 'bu ba'i bya ba byed do|| nam mkha'i khams ni sa bon la mi sgrib pa'i bya ba byed do|| dus ni sa bon 'gyur ba'i bya ba byed do|| rkyen 'di rnams med par sa bon las myu gu mngon par 'grub par mi 'gyur gyi| nam phyi rol gyi sa'i khams ma tshang ba med par gyur la de bzhin du chu dang| me dang| rlung dang| nam mkha' dang| dus kyang ma tshang ba med par gyur te| thams cad 'dus pa las sa bon 'gags pa na de las myu gu mngon par 'grub par 'gyur ro|

(1) *Paripācayati* = lit. "cooks" hence "prepares", "makes ready". **(2)** *Abhinirharati.* **(3)** *Anāvaraṇa*, here apparently meaning: "providing space (in which to grow)". See para. 35, n. 5. C: "making no obstacle for". **(4-4)** C: And with the help of season and favorable weather (there is) change. If these six conditions are sufficient, then (there is) production. If the six conditions are absent, nothing is produced. Because earth, water, fire, wind, space and time, the six conditions, are in harmony, neither excessive nor deficient, there is production. **(5)** Season (*ṛtu*) is not called a factor (*dhātu*) here, but is so called below in this para. See para. 12, n. 2. **(6)** B: *saṅgrahakṛtyaṁ*. **(7)** B. inserts: *yato'ṅkuraḥ kaṭino bhavati.* **(8)** B. inserts: *yato'ṅkuro bījān-nirgacchati.* **(9)** B: °*pariṇāmaṁ*°. **(10-10)** B. glosses. **(11)** Msl. omits *eṣu*. **(12)** Bp. omits °*abhi-*. **(13)** Msl: *tatas-teṣām*.

14. It does not occur to the earth-factor, "I perform the function of supporting the seed", and so on until: it does not occur to season, "I perform the function of transforming the seed".[1] Nor does it occur to the sprout, "I am born by way of these conditions". [2]But still, when there are these conditions, when the seed is ceasing the development of the sprout occurs.[2] And this sprout is not self-made, not made by another, not made by both,[3] not made by God, not transformed by time,[4] not derived from *prakṛti*,[5] not founded upon a single principle,[6] (yet not arisen without cause)*. [7]From the coming together of the earth, water, heat, wind, space and season factors, when the seed is ceasing the development of the sprout occurs. Thus is the conditional relation in objective conditioned arising to be seen.[7]

Bp. 578 Msl. 109 B 2.19

14. tatra pṛthivīdhātor-naivaṁ bhavati, ahaṁ bījasya dharaṇakṛtyaṁ[8] karomīti| evaṁ[9] yāvad-ṛtor-api naivaṁ bhavati,[10] ahaṁ bījasya pariṇāmanakṛtyaṁ[11] karomīti| [12] aṅkurasyāpi naivaṁ bhavati, aham-ebhiḥ pratyayair-nirvartita[13] iti| [14]atha punaḥ [15]satsu pratyayeṣu teṣu[15] bīje nirudhyamāne'ṅkurasyābhinirvṛttir-bhavati| [16] sa cāyam-aṅkuro na svayaṁkṛto na parakṛto[17] nobhayakṛto neśvaranirmito[18] na kālapariṇāmito na prakṛtisaṁbhūto[19] (na caikakāraṇādhino)[20] nāpyāhetusamutpannaḥ| [21] pṛthivyaptejovāyvākāśartudhātusamavāyāt,[22] bīje nirudhyamāne 'ṅkurasyābhinirvṛttir-bhavati| evaṁ bāhyasya pratītyasamutpādasya pratyayopanibandho draṣṭavyaḥ||

14. de la sa'i khams kyang 'di snyam du bdag gis sa bon rten pa'i bya ba bya'o snyam du mi sems so|| de bzhin du chu'i khams kyang 'di snyam du bdag gis sa bon brlan par bya'o snyam du mi sems so|| me'i khams kyang 'di snyam du bdag gis sa bon yongs su dro bar bya'o snyam du mi sems so|| rlung gi khams kyang 'di snyam du bdag gis sa bon 'bu bar bya'o snyam du mi sems so|| nam mkha'i khams kyang 'di snyam du bdag gis sa bon la mi sgrib pa'i bya ba bya'o snyam du mi sems so| dus kyang 'di snyam du bdag gis sa bon bsgyur ba'i bya ba bya'o snyam du mi sems so| sa bon yang 'di snyam du bdag gis myu gu mngon par bsgrub bo snyam du mi sems so|| myu gu yang 'di snyam du bdag ni rkyen 'di dag gis mngon par bsgrubs so snyam du mi sems mod kyi| 'on kyang rkyen 'di dag yod la sa bon 'gag pa na myu gu mngon par 'grub par 'gyur ro|| de bzhin du me tog yod na 'bras bu'i bar du yang mngon par 'grub par 'gyur te| myu gu de yang bdag gis ma byas| gzhan gyis ma byas| gnyis gas ma byas| dbang phyug gis ma byas| dus kyis ma bsgyur| rang bzhin las ma byung| rgyu med pa las kyang ma skyes te| 'on kyang sa dang| chu dang| me dang| rlung dang| nam mkha' dang| dus kyi khams rnams 'dus nas sa bon 'gag pa na myu gu mngon par 'grub par 'gyur te| de ltar phyi rol gyi rten cing 'brel bar 'byung ba rkyen dang 'brel bar blta'o||

(1) C. and T. have entire series, but C. reads: Earth-factor (etc.) does not say ... Season does not say, "I can cause production". C. then inserts: The seed does not say, "From these six conditions I produce a sprout". T. inserts similarly, see n. 12. (2-2) C: Although it does not think (that it is) produced from these many conditions, still,(it is) from the harmonious combination of many conditions that the sprout is produced. **(3)** Three corners of typical "four cornered" (*catuskoṭi*) negation (cp. Pali S2:19-20, 22). Perhaps "not arisen without cause" is intended as the fourth corner. **(4)** Rejecting time as an agent, as opposed to transformation in time. C: born from time. **(5)** According to *Sāṁkhya*, the prime substance, from which the material universe evolves, as opposed to *puruṣa*, pure consciousness. Note the confusion over the inclusion of *prakṛti* here and in para. 34. See para. 14, n. 19. **(6)** *Kāraṇa* = "cause", but translated "principle" to distinguish from *hetu*. See para. 15, n. 1. C. omits this statement. (7-7) C. has only: This is the sequential nature of the *dharma* of origination. **(8)** B: *saṅgrahakṛtyaṁ.* **(9)** B. omits. **(10)** T. includes entire series. **(11)** B: *pariṇāmaṁ.* **(12)** T. inserts: *bījasyāpi naivaṁ bhavati, aham aṅkuram abhinirvartayāmti.* **(13)** Bp., Msl: *janita.* **(14)** B. omits from here to para. 21, as one might expect of an Advaitin! **(15–15)** Bp: *satsveteṣu* (*bīje* ...). **(16)** T. inserts: *evaṁ yāvat puṣpe sati phalasyābhinirvṛttir-bhavati.* Probably out of place from para. 11. **(17)** Bp. omits *na parakṛto.* **(18)** T. repeats *byas* = *kṛto.* SF: *spruld* = *nirmito.* Cp. para. 34, n. 10. **(19)** Here, Bp., Msl. and T. all include, but see para. 34 where Bp. and Ss. omit while Mp., Msl. and T. include. **(20)** Following Bp. and considering parallel passage below in para. 34 where Bp., Mp., and Ss. agree. T. omits here, but in para. 34 reads: *akāraṇādhino* (!). Msl. reads: *nākāraṇādhino* both here and in para. 34. **(21)** T. inserts: *atha punaḥ.* **(22)** Bp. omits *dhātu*. Msl. omits *ṛtu*. T. has both.

Pāli: *kiṁ nu kho, bho gotamo, sayaṁkataṁ sukhadukkhaṁ ti ... paraṁkataṁ ... sayaṁkataṁ ca paraṁ kataṁ ... asayaṁkāraṁ aparaṁkāraṁ adiccasamuppannaṁ sukhadukkhaṁ ti. ma hevaṁ, timbarukā ti bhagavā avoca* (S2:22, cp. S2:19–20). ... *santi bhikkhave eke samaṇabrāhmaṇā evaṁ vādino evaṁ diṭṭhino yaṁ kiñcāyam purisapuggalo paṭisaṁvedeti sukhaṁ vā dukkhaṁ vā adukkhamasukkhaṁ vā sabbaṁ taṁ pubbe katahetū ti ... issaranimmānahetū ti ... ahetu appaccayā ti* (A1:173).

SF: *(rten pa'i bya) ba bya'o snyam du myi sems so| de bzhin du chu'i khams kyang 'di ltar bdag (gi)s sa bon rlan par (bya'o snyam du mi) sems so| mye'i khams kyang 'di ltar bdag gis sa bon tshos par bya'o snyam du myi sems so| rlung gi khams kyang 'di ltar bdag gis sa bon 'bu bar bya'o snyam du myi sems so| nam mkha'i khams kyang 'di ltar b(dag gis sa bon) la myi sgrib pa'i bya ba bya'o snyam du myi sems so| dus kyang 'di ltar bdag gis sa bon bsgyur ba'i bya ba bya'o snyam du myi' sems so| sa bon yang 'di ltar bdag gis myi gu mngon bar bsgrub bo snyam du myi se(ms so| myi gu ya)ng 'di ltar bdag ni rkyen 'di dag gis mngon bar bsgrubs so snyam du myi sems mod kyi 'ond kyang rkyend 'di dag yod la sa bon 'gag pa na myi gu mngon bar 'grub par 'gyur ro d(e) bzhin du me thog yod na 'bras bu'i b(ar du yang m)ngon bar 'grub par 'gyur te myi gu de yang bdag gis ma byas| pha rold kyis ma byas gnyis kas ma byas dbang pos ma spruld| dus kyis ma bsgyurd rang bzhin las ma (byung) rgyund myed pa las kyang ma s(ky)e(s te| ')ond kyang sa dang chu dang mye (dang| rlung dang| nam) mkha' dang dus kyi khams rnams 'dus pa las myi gu skye zhing 'byung bar 'gyur te| de ltar phyi rold kyi rtend cing 'brel par 'byung ba'i ...*

15. Therein objective conditioned arising is to be seen according to five principles:[1] What five? Not as eternity, not as annihilation,[2] not as transmigration (of any essence),[3] as the development of a large fruit from a small cause,[4] and as (a result) bound to be similar to that (its cause).[5]

Bp. 579 Msl. 109
15. [6]atra bāhyaḥ pratītyasamutpādaḥ[6] pañcabhiḥ kāraṇair-draṣṭavyaḥ[7]| katamaiḥ pañcabhiḥ| na śaśvatato nocchedato na saṁkrāntitaḥ, parīttahetuto vipulaphalābhinirvṛttitaḥ,[8] tatsadṛśānuprabandhataś-ceti[9]||

15. de la phyi rol gyi rten cing 'brel bar 'byung ba rnam pa lngar blta ste| lnga gang zhe na| rtag par ma yin pa dang| chad par ma yin pa dang| 'pho bar ma yin pa dang| rgyu chung du las 'bras bu chen po mngon par 'grub pa dang| de dang 'dra ba'i rgyud du'o||

(1) *Kāraṇa*, T: *rnam pa* = *ākāra* = "kind, aspect, type". See para. 14, n. 6, where T: *byed pa* = *kāraṇa* = "cause". Translated "principle" to retain the ambiguous Skt. usage, but according to T. "seen in five ways" would be better. Cp. para. 39. **(2)** In Pāli *suttas* eternalism (*sassatavāda*) and annihilationism (*ucchedavāda*) are the two extremes rejected. See S4:400 and para. 14, n.3 above. C. considers annihilationism first. **(3)** In para. 42, *na saṁkrāntitaḥ* refers to the Buddhist doctrine of rebirth, but here, it may be taken as referring to the Buddhist doctrine of *asatkāryavāda*. **(4)** C: As (a situation in which) sprouts and seeds are few, (but) fruits are many. **(5)** C: Like is succeeded by like (and) does not produce different things. **(6-6)** Bp: *tatra samutpāda*. **(7)** T: *rnam pa* = *ākāra* = "kind". Cp. para. 14 where T: *byed pa* = *kāraṇa*. **(8)** Bp: *hetuphala*°, which VP corrects. **(9)** Bp. omits *pra-*.

16. How is it (to be seen) as "not eternity"? Because the sprout is one (thing) and the seed another. That which is the seed is not the sprout. But still, the seed ceases, and the sprout arises. Therefore eternity is not (the case).[1]

Bp. 579 Msl. 109
16. Kathaṁ na śāśvatata iti| yasmād-anyo 'ṅkuro 'nyad-bījaṁ| na ca yad-eva bījaṁ sa evāṅkuraḥ| [2] atha vā[3] punar-bījaṁ nirudhyate, [4] aṅkuraś-cotpadyate| ato na śāśvatataḥ||

16. ji ltar rtag par ma yin zhe na| gang gi phyir myu gu yang gzhan la sa bon yang gzhan te| myu gu gang yin pa de nyid sa bon ma yin la| sa bon 'gags pa las myu gu 'byung ba ma yin| ma 'gags pa las kyang ma yin gyi| sa bon yang 'gag la de nyid kyi tshe myu gu'ang 'byung ste| de'i phyir rtag par ma yin no||

(1) C., confusing paras. 16 and 17, reads: Why is it not annihilation? Because from the seed, the sprout, root, and stem arise in sequence and continuity, annihilation is not (the case). (See para. 17, n. 2). **(2)** T. inserts: *na niruddhād-bījād-aṅkura utpadyate nāpy-āniruddhād-bījād*. Out of place from para. 17? (See para. 17, n. 4). **(3)** Msl: *atha-ca*. **(4)** T. inserts: *tasminneva samaye*. Out of place from para. 17?

17. How is it (to be seen) as "not annihilation"? Not from the previous cessation of the seed does the sprout issue forth, nor indeed without the cessation of the seed. But still the seed ceases, and at just that time[1] the sprout arises, like the beam of a scale rocking to and fro. Therefore annihilation is not (the case).[2]

Bp. 579 Msl. 109
17. Kathaṁ [3] nocchedataḥ| na ca pūrvaniruddhād-bījād-aṅkuro niṣpadyate, nāpy-aniruddhād-bījāt[4]| api ca| bījaṁ ca nirudhyate, tasminneva samaye 'ṅkura utpadyate, tulādaṇḍonnāmāvanāmavat| ato nocchedataḥ||

17. ji ltar chad par ma yin zhe na| sngon 'gags pa'i sa bon las myu gu skye ba ma yin| ma 'gags pa las kyang ma yin gyi| sa bon yang 'gag la de nyid kyi tshe srang mda'i mtho dman bzhin du myu gu skye bas de'i phyir chad par ma yin no||

(1) Note the resemblance to the doctrine of momentariness (*kṣaṇikavāda*). See Stcherbatsky, *Buddhist Logic I*, pp. 79ff. **(2)** For para. 17, C: Why is it not eternal? Sprout, stem, flower and fruit are all distinct, therefore it is not eternal. Neither is it that the seed ceases and afterwards the sprout arises, nor is it that (it) does not expire and the sprout arises. But (by) the *dharma* of cause and condition, the sprout grows (when) the seed fades. Because of the sequentiality of arising eternity is not (the case). (See para. 16, n. 1). **(3)** Msl. inserts: *punar*. **(4)** See para. 16, n. 2.

18. How is it (to be seen) as "not transmigration"? The seed and sprout are dissimilar.[1] Therefore transmigration is not (the case).[2]

Bp. 579 Msl. 109
18. kathaṁ na saṁkrāntitaḥ| [3]visadṛśo bījād-aṅkura iti,[3] ato na saṁkrāntitaḥ||

18. ji ltar 'pho bar ma yin zhe na| gang gi phyir myu gu yang gzhan la sa bon yang gzhan| myu gu gang yin pa de nyid sa bon ma yin te| de'i phyir 'pho bar ma yin no||

(1) Similarity to para. 16 emphasizes the similarity of these two rejected views. **(2)** For para. 18, C: Because seed and sprout differ in name and characteristics (transmigration) from this to that is not (the case). **(3-3)** T. repeats with minor changes from para. 16.

19. How is it (to be seen) as the development of a large fruit from a small cause? "A small seed is sown, and it causes a large fruit to develop." Therefore it is (to be seen) as the development of a large fruit from a small cause.[1]

Bp. 579 Msl. 109
19. kathaṁ parīttahetuto vipulaphalābhinirvṛttitaḥ| parīttabījam-upyate vipulaphalābhinirvartayatīti[2]| ataḥ parīttahetuto vipulaphalābhinirvṛttitaḥ||

19. ji ltar rgyu chung du las 'bras bu chen po mngon par 'grub ce na| sa bon chung du btab pa las 'bras bu chen po mngon par 'grub par 'gyur te| de'i phyir rgyu chung du las 'bras bu chen po mngon par 'grub bo||

(1) For para. 19, C: Because seeds are few (but) fruits are many one should know (these) are not the same. This is what is meant by, "The seeds are few (but) the fruits are many". (2) T. omits *iti*.

20. How is it (to be seen) as (a result) bound to be similar to that (its cause)? "Whatever type of seed is sown, it causes that type of fruit to develop." Therefore it is (to be seen) as (a result) bound to be similar to that (its cause). Thus is objective conditioned arising to be seen according to five principles.[1]

Bp. 579 Msl. 109
20. kathaṁ tatsadṛśānuprabandhataḥ| yādṛśaṁ bījam-upyate tādṛśaṁ phalam-abhinirvartayatīti[2]| atas-tatsadṛśānuprabandhataś-ceti|| evaṁ bāhyaḥ pratītyasamutpādaḥ pañcabhiḥ kāraṇair-draṣṭavyaḥ||[3]

20. sa bon ji lta bu btab pa de lta bu'i 'bras bu mngon par 'grub pas de'i phyir de dang 'dra ba'i rgyud du ste| de ltar phyi rol gyi rten cing 'brel bar 'byung ba rnam pa lngar blta'o||

(1) For para. 20, C: Because a seed does not produce a different fruit it is called similar and continuous. With these five kinds of external conditions, all things are born. (2) T. omits *iti*. (3) Bp. 576-579 citation ends here.

21. Thus subjective conditioned arising also arises from two principles. From what two? From a causal relation and a conditional relation.[1]

Mp. 560 B. 2.19

21. evam-ādhyātmiko'pi[2] pratītyasamutpādo dvābhyām-eva[3] kāraṇābhyām-utpadyate[4]| katamābhyāṁ dvābhyām|[5] [6] hetūpanibandhataḥ pratyayopanibandhataś-ca|

21. de bzhin du nang gi rten cing 'brel bar 'byung ba yang gnyis kyi phyir 'byung ste| gnyis gang zhe na| 'di lta ste| rgyu dang 'brel ba dang| rkyen dang 'brel ba'o||

(1) For para. 21, C. has only: Internal caused and conditioned *dharma(s)* are produced from two principles. (2) B: *tatrādhyātmikaḥ.* (3) B. omits. (4) B: *bhavati.* (5) B. omits. (6) T. inserts: *tadyathā.*

22. What, then, is the causal relation in subjective conditioned arising? It is as follows:[1] Ignorance conditions (mental) formations. (Mental) formations condition consciousness. Consciousness conditions name-and-form. Name-and-form conditions the six (sense) entrances. The six (sense) entrances condition contact. Contact conditions sensation. Sensation conditions desire. Desire conditions grasping. Grasping conditions becoming. Becoming conditions birth. Brith conditions decay and death, and grief, lamentation, suffering, depression and anxiety come to be. Thus the arising of this entire great mass of suffering occurs. Were there no ignorance, (mental) formations would not be known, and so on until: were there no birth, decay and death would not be known. But when there is ignorance, the development of (mental) formations occurs, and so on until: when there is birth, the development of decay and death occurs. Herein, it does not occur to ignorance,[2] "I cause the (mental) formations to develop". Nor does it occur to the (mental) formations, "We are developed by ignorance", and so on until: it does not occur to birth, "I develop decay and death"[3] Nor does it occur to decay and death, "I am developed by birth". But still, when there is ignorance, the development, the manifestation of (mental) formations occurs, and so on until: when there is birth, the development, the manifestation of decay and death occurs. Thus is the causal relation in subjective conditioned arising to be seen.[4]

Mp. 560 Ss. 219 Msl. 110 B. 2.19

22. tatrādhyatmikasya[5] pratītyasamutpādasya hetūpanibandhaḥ katamo|[6] yadidam-avidyapratyayāḥ saṁskārāḥ, [7]saṁskārapratyayaṁ vijñānaṁ, vijñānapratyayaṁ nāmarūpaṁ, nāmarūpapratyayaṁ ṣaḍāyatanaṁ, ṣaḍāyatanapratyayaḥ sparśaḥ, sparśapratyayā vedanā, vedanapratyayā tṛṣṇā| tṛṣṇāpratyayam-upādānaṁ, upādānapratyayo bhavo, bhavapratyayā jātiḥ, jātipratyayā jarāmaraṇaśokaparidevaduḥkhadaurmanasyopāyāsāḥ saṁbhavanti| evam-asya kevalasya mahato duḥkhaskandhasya samudayo bhavati|[7] avidyā cennābhaviṣyan-naiva saṁskārāḥ prajñāsyante,[8] evaṁ [9]yāvaj-jātiś-cennābhaviṣyaj-jarāmaraṇaṁ na[9] prajñāsyante| atha vā[10] satyām avidyāyāṁ saṁskārāṇām-abhinirvṛttir bhavati, evaṁ yāvaj-jātyāṁ satyāṁ[11] jarāmaraṇa-

syābhinirvṛttir-bhavati||[12] tatrāvidyāyā[13] naivaṁ bhavati, ahaṁ saṁskārān-abhinirvartayāmīti| [14] saṁskārāṇām-api naivaṁ[15] bhavati, vayam-avidyayābhinirvartitā[16] iti| evaṁ yāvaj-jāter[17]api naivaṁ bhavati, ahaṁ jarāmaraṇam-abhinirvartayāmīti[18]| jarāmaraṇasyāpi[19] naivaṁ bhavaty-ahaṁ jātyābhinirvartitam-iti[20]|| [21]atha ca satyām-avidyāyāṁ saṁskārāṇām-abhinirvṛttir-bhavati prādurbhāvaḥ[22]| evaṁ yāvaj-jātyāṁ satyaṁ jarāmaraṇasyābhinirvṛttir-bhavati prādurbhāvaḥ[23]| evam-ādhyātmikasya pratītyasamutpādasya hetūpanibandho draṣṭavyaḥ||[21]

22. de la nang gi rten cing 'brel bar 'byung ba rgyu dang 'brel ba gang zhe na| gang 'di ma rig pa'i rkyen gyis 'du byed rnams zhes bya ba nas skye ba'i rkyen gyis rga shi zhes bya ba'i bar du'o|| gal te ma rig pa ma byung na 'du byed rnams kyang mi mngon pa zhig| de bzhin du skye ba ma byung du zin na rga shi'i bar du yang mi mngon pa zhig na| 'di ltar ma rig pa yod pa las 'du byed rnams mngon par 'grub par 'gyur ba nas skye ba yod pa las rga shi'i bar du mngon par 'grub par 'gyur ro|| de la ma rig pa yang 'di snyam du bdag gis 'du byed rnams mngon par bsgrub bo snyam du mi sems so|| 'du byed rnams kyang 'di snyam du bdag cag ni ma rig pas mngon par bsgrubs so snyam du mi sems pa nas de bzhin du skye ba yang 'di snyam du bdag gis rga shi mngon par bsgrub bo snyam du mi sems shing| rga shi yang 'di snyam du bdag ni skye bas mngon par bsgrubs so snyam du mi sems pa'i bar du ste| 'on kyang ma rig pa yod pa las 'du byed rnams mngon par 'grub cing 'byung bar 'gyur ba nas de bzhin du skye ba yod pa las rga shi'i bar du mngon par 'grub cing 'byung bar 'gyur te| de ltar nang gi rten cing 'brel bar 'byung ba rgyu dang 'brel bar blta'o||

(1) C. has only: What is cause? **(2)** C: Ignorance (etc.) does not say ... **(3)** In course of ellipsis, C. omits: it ... birth. **(4)** C: This is called internal cause in the sequential *dharma* of origination. **(5)** Msl: *tatra punaś-cādhy°*. **(6)** B: *tatrāsya hetūpanibandho.* **(7-7)** Ss., Msl: *yāvaj-jātipratyayaṁ jarāmaraṇam-iti|*, as B, but B: *°maraṇād°*. C. also omits with elipsis. **(8)** B: *ajaniṣyanta.* **(9-9)** Ss: *yāvadyadi jātir nābhaviṣyan na jarāmaraṇam.* Msl. as Ss., but: *°syat skandhānāṁ pañcānaṁ prādurbhāvo jātiriti tatra jarāmaranaṁ na.* B: *yāvaj-jātiḥ, jātiś-cennābhaviṣyan-naivaṁ jarāmaraṇādaya udapatsyanta|.* **(10)** Ss. omits. Msl: *ca.* **(11)** Mp. omits. **(12)** Msl. omits. **(13)** Mp: *atra.* **(14)** Msl. inserts: *punaḥ.* **(15)** Ss., Msl: *apy-evam na.* **(16)** Ss: *°vṛttā.* **(17)** Ss: *°jatyā (naivaṁ).* B: *°jātyā (api).* Msl: *°jāteḥ skandhaprādurbhāvasya (naivam ...).* **(18)** B: *jarāmaraṇādyābhi°.* **(19)** B: *jarāmaraṇādīnām-api.* **(20)** Mp: *°yānirvartitam°.* Ss: *°yānirvṛtta iti|.* **(21-21)** B. replaces with explanatory material irrelevant to text. **(22)** Msl: *prādurbhāva evaṁ, (evam yāvat ...).* **(23)** Msl: *°vṛttiḥ prādurbhāvo bhavati.*

Pāli: *jātiyā kho sati jarāmaraṇaṁ hoti jātipaccayā jarāmaraṇaṁ ti. ... avijjāya kho sati sankhārā honti avijjā paccayā sankhārāti ... jatiyā kho asati jarāmaraṇaṁ na hoti jātinirodhā jarāmaraṇanirodho ti. ... avijjāya kho asati sankhārā na honti avijjānirodhā sankharanirodho ti* (S2:10-11).

23. How is the conditional relation in subjective conditioned arising to be seen? As due to the coming together of six factors. As due to the coming together of what six factors? Namely as due to the coming together of the earth, water, heat, wind, space and consciousness factors[1] is the conditional relation in subjective conditioned arising to be seen.[2]

Mp. 561 Ss. 220 Msl. 110 B. 2.19
23. [3]kathām[4]-ādhyātmikasya pratītyasamutpādasya pratyayopanibandho draṣṭavya iti, [5]ṣaṇṇām dhātūnāṁ samavāyāt| katameṣāṁ ṣaṇṇāṁ dhātūnāṁ samavāyāt|[5] yadidaṁ[3] pṛthivyaptejovāyvākāśavijñānadhātūnāṁ samavāyād [6]ādhyatmikasya pratītyasamutpādasya pratyayopanibandho draṣṭavyaḥ[6]||

23. nang gi rten cing 'brel bar 'byung ba rkyen dang 'brel bar ji ltar blta zhe na| khams drug 'dus pa'i phyir te| khams drug po gang dag 'dus pa'i phyir zhe na| 'di lta ste| sa dang| chu dang| me dang| rlung dang| nam mka' dang| rnam par shes pa'i khams rnams 'dus pa las nang gi rten cing 'brel bar 'byung ba rkyen dang 'brel bar blta'o||

(1) Here the standard list of six *dhātus* (see para. 12, n. 27) as in A1:176; S3: 230, 248; D3:247; 274; M3:31; Vbh. 85, 87. Note that in the *Śālistamba, vijñāna* is both a cause (para. 22) and a condition (para. 23), an inconsistency resulting from trying to combine separate formulas (i.e. the six *dhātus* and *pratītyasamutpāda*) into a more unified whole. See also S3:10, where the five aggregates (*khanda*) are called *dhātu*. **(2)** For para. 23, C: What is called internal condition (in the) *dharma* of origination? (It is) the so-called six factors: earth ... consciousness factors. **(3-3)** B: *atha pratyayopanibandhaḥ*. **(4)** Msl: *punaḥ katham*. **(5-5)** Ss., Msl. omit. Cp. para. 12, where Bp., Msl. include. **(6-6)** B: *bhavati kāyaḥ*|.

SF: (*khams drug po*) *dang gang 'dus pa'i phyir zhe na ...*

24. [1]Therein, what is the earth-factor in subjective conditioned arising? That which, by conglomeration, causes the solid nature of the body to develop, is called the earth-factor. That which performs the cohesion-function of the body is called the water-factor. That which digests what is eaten, drunk or consumed for the body is called the heat-factor. That which performs the body's function of inhalation and exhalation is called the wind-factor. That which causes hollowness to develop inside the body is called the space-factor. That which causes name-and-form to develop (mutually supported) like reeds in a sheaf[2] is called the consciousness-factor, associated with the five consciousness bodies[3] and defiled mind-consciousness.[4] Without these conditions, the arising of the body does not occur. But if the subjective earth-factor is not deficient, and likewise the water, heat, wind, space and consciousness factors are not deficient, then, because of all these factors coming together, the arising of the body occurs.

Mp. 561 Ss. 220 Msl. 110 B. 2.19
24.[5] tatrādhyātmikasya pratītyasamutpādasya pṛthivīdhātuḥ katamo,[6] yaḥ[7] kāyasya saṁśleṣāt-kaṭhinabhāvam-abhinirvartayati,[8] ayam ucyate pṛthivīdhātuḥ| yaḥ[9] kāyasyānuparigrahakṛtyaṁ[10] karoti, ayam-ucyate'bdhātuḥ| yaḥ[11] kāyasyāśītapītabhakṣitaṁ[12] paripācayati, ayam-ucyate tejodhātuḥ| yaḥ kāyasya āśvāsapraśvāsakṛtyaṁ [13] karoty-ayam-ucyate vāyudhātuḥ| yaḥ kāyasyāntaḥ śauṣīryam[14]-abhinirvartayati, ayam ucyate ākāśadhātuḥ| yo [15] nāmarūpam[16] abhinirvartayati naḍakalāpayogena, pañcavijñānakāyasaṁyuktaṁ[17] sāsravaṁ [18] ca manovijñānaṁ, ayam-ucyate bhikṣavo[19] vijñānadhātuḥ|| [20]tatrāsatām-eṣāṁ pratyayānāṁ[20] kāyasyotpattir-na bhavati| yadā tv-ādhyātmikaḥ[21] pṛthivīdhātur-avikalo bhavati, evam-aptejovāyvākāśavijñānadhātavaścāvikalā[22] bhavanti, tataḥ[23] sarveṣāṁ samavāyāt-kāyasyotpattirbhavati[24]||

24. de la nang gi rten cing 'brel bar 'byung ba'i sa'i khams gang zhe na| gang 'di 'dus nas lus kyi sra ba'i dngos po mngon par 'grub par byed pa 'di ni sa'i khams shes bya'o|| gang lus sdud pa'i bya ba byed pa 'di ni chu'i khams shes bya'o|| gang lus kyis zos pa dang| 'thungs pa dang| 'chos pa dang| myangs pa rnams 'ju bar byed pa 'di ni me'i khams shes bya'o|| gang lus kyi dbugs phyi nang du rgyu ba'i bya ba byed pa 'di ni rlung gi khams shes bya'o|| gang lus kyi nang sbubs yod par byed pa 'di ni nam mkha'i khams shes bya'o|| gang mdung khyim gyi tshul du lus kyi ming dang gzugs kyi myu gu mngon par 'grub par byed pa rnam par shes pa'i tshogs lnga 'dus pa dang| zag pa dang bcas pa'i yid kyi rnam par shes pa gang yin pa 'di ni rnam par shes pa'i khams shes bya'o|| rkyen 'di dag med par lus skye bar mi 'gyur gyi| nam nang gi sa'i khams tshang zhing de bzhin du chu dang| me dang| rlung dang| nam mkha' dang| rnam par shes pa'i khams rnams kyang tshang bar gyur la| thams cad 'dus pa de las lus mngon par 'grub par 'gyur ro||

(1) For para. 24, C: What is known as earth? (That which) can firmly support is called earth-factor. What is known as water? (That which) can moisten and soak is called water-factor. What is known as heat? (That which) can ripen (i.e. digest) is called heat-factor. What is known as wind? (That which) can cause inhalation and exhalation is called wind-factor. What is known as space? (That which) can (create) absence of obstacles is called space-factor. What is known as consciousness? Four *skandhas* and five (sense) consciousnesses are said to be name, and are called consciousness. Similarly, many elements (*dharma*) put together are called body. Defiled mind is called consciousness. Thus, four *skandhas* are five (sensory) feelings, whose bases are called form. Similarly, six conditions are known as body. If (these) six conditions are sufficient, not deficient, the body is formed. If the conditions are deficient, the body is not formed. **(2)** Referring to the mutual dependence of *nāmarūpa* and *vijñāna* which is more specifically stated in some Pāli passages (S2:114). **(3)** *vijñāna-kāya*, probably = "types of (sensual) consciousness (comprised of organ, object and appropriate consciousness)". See D3:243; M3:281; *Artha-viniścaya*, para. 5 and comy. (Patna ed., p. 8). Cp. para. 27, n. 8. **(4)** *sāsravaṁ manovijñānam*. Cp. M1:7, D2:81, Asl. 48. **(5)** B. glosses para. 24, only variation being: *abdhātuḥ snehayati kāyam*. **(6)** Ss., Msl: *katama iti*. **(7)** Ss., and Msl. *yo'yam*. **(8)** Ss: *saṁśleṣataḥ kaṭhina°*. Msl: *saṁśleṣataḥ saṁparkāt kaṭhina°*. **(9)** Msl: *yaḥ punaḥ*. **(10)** Msl: *kāyasya parigrahakṛtyaṃ svīkārasaṁcayakṛtyaṁ*. **(11)** Msl: *yaś-ca punaḥ*. **(12)** Following Ss., Mp: *āśītabhakṣitaṁ*. Msl: *āśītaṁ pītaṁ bhakśitaṁ*. T: *āśitapītabhakṣitakhāditaṁ*. Cp. para. 25, n. 7. **(13)** Msl. inserts: *vāyor-ākarṣaṇam-āśvāsaḥ etat-kṛtyaṁ*. **(14)** Ss., Msl: *śauṣīryabhāvam*. **(15)** T. inserts: *kāyasya*. **(16)** T: *°rupāṅkuram*. **(17)** Ss: *°saṁprayuktam*. Msl: *naḍakālāpayogena cakṣur-ādi-pañcavidhavijñānakāya vijñānasamūhasaṁuktaṁ*. **(18)** Msl. inserts: *sāvaraṇaṁ*. **(19)** Ss., Msl. omit. **(20-20)** Ss., Msl: *asatsu pratyayeṣu*. **(21)** Ss: *yadādhy°*. Msl: *yadā cādhy°*. **(22)** Msl: *°vāyuvijñānākāśa°*. **(23)** Msl: *tatasteṣāṁ*. **(24)** T: *°kāyasyābhinirvṛttir°*.

Pāli: *yaṁ kiñci rāhula ajjhattaṁ paccattaṁ kakkhaḷaṁ kharigatam upādiṇṇaṁ ... ayaṁ vuccati rāhula ajjhattikā paṭhavīdhātu. yā c'eva kho pana ajjhattikā paṭhavīdhātu yā ca bāhirā paṭhavīdhātu paṭhavīdhāturevesā ... apodhātu siyā ajjhattikā siyā bāhirā ... yaṁ ajjhattaṁ paccattaṁ āpo āpogataṁ upādiṇṇaṁ ... ayaṁ vuccati rāhula ajjhattikā āpodhātu ... yaṁ ajjhattaṁ paccattaṁ tejo tejogataṁ upādiṇṇaṁ, seyyathīdaṁ yena ca santappati yena ca jiriyati yena ca pariḍayhati yena ca asitapītakhāyitasāyitam sammā pariṇāmaṁ gaccati ... ayam vuccati rāhula ajjhattikā tejodhātu ... yaṁ ajjhattaṁ paccattaṁ vāyo vāyogataṁ upādiṇṇaṁ, seyyathīdaṁ ... assāso passāso iti ... ayaṁ vuccati rāhula ajjhattikā vāyodhātu ... yaṁ ajjhattaṁ paccattaṁ ākāsaṁ ākāsagataṁ upadiṇṇaṁ, seyyathīdaṁ kaṇṇacchiddaṁ nāsacchiddaṁ mukhadvāraṁ ... ayaṁ vuccati rāhula ajjhattikā ākāsadhātu. yā c' eva kho pana ajjhattikā ākāsadhātu yā ca bāhirā ākāsadhātu ākāsadhāturevesā* (M1:421-23).

SF: *...byed pa 'di ni sa'i kham(s) shes bya'o ... (gang lus kyi dbugs) phyi nang du rgyu ba'i bya ba byed pa 'di ni (rlung) ... (tshogs) lnga dang ldan ba dang| zag pa dang bcas ... (rnam par shes) pa'i khams kyang tshang bar gyur ...*

25. [1]Therein, it does not occur to the earth-factor, "I cause the solid nature of the body to develop". Nor does it occur to the water-factor, "I perform the cohesion-function of the body". Nor does it occur to the heat-factor, "I digest what is eaten, drunk or consumed for the body". Nor does it occur to the wind-factor, "I perform the body's function of inhalation and exhalation". Nor does it occur to the space-factor, "I cause hollowness to develop inside the body". Nor does it occur to the consciousness-factor, "I cause the body to develop".[1] Nor does it occur to the body, "I am born by way of these conditions". [2]But still, when there are these conditions, because of their coming together, the arising of the body occurs.[2]

Mp. 562 Ss. 221 Msl. 111 B. 2.19

25. [3]tatra pṛthivīdhātor-naivaṁ bhavaty-ahaṁ[4] kāyasya [5] kaṭhinabhāvam-abhinirvartayāmīti| abdhātor-naivaṁ bhavaty-ahaṁ kāyasyānuparigrahakṛtyaṁ[6] karomīti| tejodhātor-naivaṁ bhavaty-ahaṁ kāyasyāśitapītakhāditaṁ[7] paripācayāmīti| vāyudhātornaivaṁ bhavaty-ahaṁ kāyasyāśvāsapraśvāsakṛtyaṁ karomīti| ākāśadhātor-naivaṁ bhavaty-ahaṁ kāyasyāntaḥ-śauṣīryam-abhinirvartayāmīti[8]| [9] vijñānadhtor-naivaṁ bhavaty-ahaṁ [10]kāyam[11]-abhinirvartayāmīti|[3] [12]kāyasyāpi naivaṁ bhavaty-aham-[10] ebhiḥ pratyayair-janita iti|[12] atha ca punaḥ satām-eṣaṁ pratyayānāṁ samavāyāt-kāyasyotpattir-bhavati|[13]

25. de la sa'i khams kyang 'di snyam du bdag gis 'dus nas lus kyi sra ba'i dngos po mngon par bsgrub bo snyam du mi sems so|| chu'i khams kyang 'di snyam du bdag gis lus kyi sdud pa'i bya ba bya'o snyam du mi sems so|| me'i khams kyang 'di snyam du bdag gis lus kyi zos pa dang| 'thungs pa dang| 'chos pa dang| myangs pa rnams 'ju bar bya'o snyam du mi sems so|| rlung gi khams kyang 'di snyam du bdag gis lus kyi dbugs phyi nang du rgyu ba'i bya ba bya'o snyam du mi sems so|| nam mkha'i khams kyang 'di snyam du bdag gis lus kyi nang sbubs yod par bya'o snyam du mi sems so|| rnam par shes pa'i khams kyang 'di snyam du bdag gis lus kyi ming dang gzugs mngon par 'grub bo snyam du mi sems so|| lus kyang 'di snyam du bdag ni rkyen 'di dag gis bskyed do snyam du mi sems mod kyi|| 'on kyang rkyen 'di dag yod na lus skye bar 'gyur ro||

Para. 25:
(1-1) C: Earth does not think ... water ... fire ... wind ... space ... consciousness does not think ... "I can sustain" ... "I can water" ... "I can ripen" ... "I can cause inhalation and exhalation" ... "I can cause absence of obstacles" ... "I can cause birth and growth". **(2-2)** C: If there are not these six conditions, the body is not born. **(3-3)** B: *tatra pṛthivyādidhātūnāṁ naivam bhavati vayam kāyasya kāṭinyādi nirvartayāma iti.* **(4)** Ss., Msl. consistently read: *bhavati, ahaṁ ....* **(5)** T. inserts: *saṁśleṣāt.* **(6)** Mp: *°ānugraha°*. **(7)** All Skt. sources read *khāditam* instead of *bhakṣitaṁ*. T. has both. Cp. para. 24, n. 12. **(8)** Ss: *śauṣīryaṁ karomīti.* Msl: *°śauṣīryabhavam°*. **(9)** Mp. inserts: *ṛtor-api naivaṁ bhavaty-ahaṁ kāyasya pariṇamanākṛtyaṁ karomīti|* **(10-10)** Ss. omits. **(11)** T: *kāyasya nāmarūpam°*. **(12-12)** Msl: *pratyayaviśeṣair-janita iti.* B: *... bhavati jñānam-aham-ebhiḥ pratyayair-abhinirvartita iti.* **(13)** Ss: *atha ca sastv-eṣu pratyayeṣu kāyasyotpattir-bhavati|* Msl. as Ss., but: *°satsu praty°*. B: *atha ca pṛthivyādidhātubhyo'cetanebhyaś-cetanātarānadhiṣṭhitebhyoṅkurasy-eva kāyasyotpatiḥ, so 'yam pratītyasamutpādo dṛṣṭavānnānyathayitavyaḥ.*

SF: ... *(s)nyam du myi sems so| mye'i khams kya(ng) ... ('thungs) pa dang 'chos (pa dang) myangs pa rnams 'dzu (bar bya'o) snyam du myi sems so| rlung gi kham(s) ... nam mkha'i khams kyang 'di ltar bdag (gis lus kyi ... mi se)ms so| rnam par shes pa'i khams kyang '(di ltar) bdag gis lus mngon du 'grub pa(r) ... (lus ... rkyen 'di dag gis) bskyed do snyam du myi sems mod kyi ... (lus 'byu)ng bar 'gyur ro|*

26. Therein, the earth-factor is [1]not self, not a being, not a soul, not a creature, not human, not a person, not female, not male, not neuter, not "I", not "mine", and not any other's. Likewise the water-factor, heat-factor, wind-factor, space-factor, and consciousness-factor are not self, not a being, not a soul, not a creature, not human, not a person, not female, not male, not neuter, not "I", not "mine", and not any other's.[1]

Mp. 562 Ss. 221 Msl. 111
26. tatra pṛthivīdhātur-nātmā na sattvo[2] na jīvo na jantur-na manujo na mānavo na strī na pumān-na[3] napuṁsakaṁ na cāhaṁ na [4] mama na cānyasya[5] kasyacit| [6]evam-abdhātus-tejodhātur-vāyudhātur-ākāśadhātur-vijñānadhātur-nātmā[7] na sattvo na jīvo na jantur-na manujo na mānavo na strī na pumān-na[8] napuṁsakaṁ na cāhaṁ na mama na cānyasya[9] kasyacit||[6]

26. de la sa'i khams ni bdag ma yin| sems can ma yin| srog ma yin| skye ba po ma yin| shed las skyes pa ma yin| shed bu ma yin| bud med ma yin| skyes pa ma yin| ma ning ma yin| nga ma yin| bdag gi ma yin te| gzhan su'i yang ma yin no|| de bzhin du chu'i khams dang| me'i khams dang| rlung gi khams dang nam mkha'i khams dang| rnam par shes pa'i khams kyang bdag ma yin| sems can ma yin| srog ma yin| skye ba po ma yin| shed las skyes pa ma yin| shed bu ma yin| bud med ma yin| skyes pa ma yin| ma ning ma yin| nga ma yin| bdag gi ma yin| gzhan su'i yang ma yin no||

Para. 26: **(1-1)** C: ... not self, not a person, not (any of the) many beings, not a life, not male, not female, not neuter, not this and not that. **(2)** Msl: °*nātmā na mukto na badho (na jīvo ...)*. **(3)** Msl. and T: *na strī na purūṣo na napuṁsakaṁ.* **(4)** Msl. inserts *ca.* **(5)** Ss: *na cāpy-anyasya.* Msl: *nāpy-anyasya.* **(6-6)** Msl. omits. **(7)** Ss. omits *nātmā.* Mp: °*ākāśadhātur-ṛtudhātur-vijñāna*°. **(8)** T. as above, n. 3. **(9)** Ss: *na cāpy-anyasya.*

Pāli: (cont. from para. 24) *taṁ netaṁ mama, nesohamasmi, na meso attā ti* (M1:421-23).

SF: *de la sa'i khams bdag ma (yi)n| sems can ma yin (sr)o(g ma yin) ... (bud med ma) yin| skyes pa ma yin| ma ning ma (yin) ... (gzhan su'i yang) ma yin no| de bzhin du chu'i khams dang mye'i (khams) dang rlung gi (khams) ... (sems can) ma yin| srog ma yin| skye ba ma yin| ... (bud me)d ma yin| skyes pa ma yin| ma ning ma yin| ... (gzhan su'i) yang ma yi(n no||)*

27.[1] Therein, what is ignorance? That which perceives these same six factors as a unit, as a lump, as permanent, as constant, as eternal, as pleasant, as self, as a being, a soul, a person, a human, a man, as making "I"[2] or making "mine" and so on into manifold misapprehension, that is called ignorance. When there is this ignorance, greed, hatred and delusion[3] develop in (relation to) the (sense) spheres.[4] Greed, hatred and delusion in (relation to) the (sense) spheres are called (mental) formations. The discrete appearance of objects[5] is consciousness. The four non-material grasping-aggregates which arise together with consciousness are name. (Name) together with the four great elements and derived matter is name-and-form. The (sense) faculties connected with name-and-form are the six (sense) entrances. The conjunction of three things is contact.[6] The experience of contact is sensation. Clinging to sensation is desire. The expansion of desire is grasping. Action, born out of grasping and giving rise to rebirth, is becoming. The manifestation of the aggregates caused by becoming is birth. The maturing of the born aggregates is decay. The perishing of the worn out aggregates is death. The internal burning[7] of the deluded, attached, dying (person) is grief. Giving vent to grief is lamentation. The experience of unpleasantness associated with the five consciousness bodies[8] is suffering. Mental suffering associated with the mind[9] is depression. And whatever other subtle defilements[10] there are of this sort are anxiety.

Mp. 562 Ss. 221 Bp. 387 Msl. 111 B. 2.19

27. tatrāvidyā katamā, [11]yaiṣām-eva ṣaṇṇāṁ dhātūnām-aikya saṁjñā[11] piṇḍasaṁjñā nityasaṁjñā [12]dhruvasaṁjñā śāśvatasaṁjñā[12] sukhasaṁjñā [13]ātmasaṁjñā sattvasaṁjñā jīvapudgalamanujamānavasaṁjñā[13] [14]ahaṁkāramamakārasaṁjñā| evam-ādi-vividham-ajñānam[14]-iyaṁ-ucyate 'vidyeti|| evam-avidyāyāṁ satyāṁ viṣayeṣu rāgadveṣamohāḥ pravartante| tatra ye rāgadveṣamohā viṣayeṣv-amī saṁskārā ity-ucyante|[15] vastuprativijñaptir vijñānaṁ|[16] vijñānasahajāś-catvāro 'rūpina upādānaskandhās-tan-nāma, catvāri ca mahābhūtāni copādāya upādāya rūpam-aikadhayam-abhisaṁkṣipya tan-nāmarūpaṁ|[17] nāmarūpasaṁniśritānīndriyāṇi ṣaḍāyatanaṁ|[18] trayāṇaṁ dharmāṇāṁ saṁnipātaḥ sparśaḥ|[19] sparśānubhavo vedanā|[20] vedanādhyavasānaṁ tṛṣṇā|[21] tṛṣṇāvaipulyam-upādānaṁ|[22] upādānanirjātaṁ punarbhavajanakaṁ karma bhavaḥ|[23] bhavahetukaḥ[24] skandhaprādurbhāvo jātiḥ[25]| jātasya skandhaparipāko jarā|[26] jīrṇasya skandhasya vinaśo maraṇaṁ|[27] mriyamāṇasya saṁmūḍhasya[28] sābhiṣvaṅgasyāntardāhaḥ śokaḥ|[29] śokotthamālāpanaṁ paridevaḥ|[30] pañcavijñānakāyasaṁyuktam-asātam-anubhavanaṁ[31] duḥkaṁ| manasā saṁyuktaṁ[32] mānasaṁ [33] duḥkhaṁ daurmanasyaṁ| ye cāpy-anya[34] evam-ādaya [35] upakleśāste upāyāsā iti||[36]

27. de la ma rig pa gang zhe na| khams drug po 'di dag nyid la gang gcig pur 'du shes pa dang| ril por 'du shes pa dang| rtag par 'du shes pa dang| brtan par 'du shes pa dang| ther zug tu 'du shes pa dang| bde bar 'du shes pa dang| bdag tu 'du shes pa dang| sems can dang| srog dang| skyes ba po dang| gso ba dang| skyes bu dang| gang zag tu 'du shes pa dang| shed las skye pa dang| shed bur 'du shes pa dang| nga zhes bya ba dang| bdag gi zhes bya bar 'du shes pa ste| 'di lta bu la sogs pa mi shes pa rnam pa sna tshogs 'di ni ma rig pa zhes bya'o|| de ltar ma rig pa yod pas yul rnams la 'dod chags dang| zhe sdang dang| gti mug 'jug ste| de la yul rnams la 'dod chags dang| zhe sdang dang| gti mug gang yin pa 'di ni ma rig pa'i rkyen gyis 'du byed rnams zhes bya'o| dngos po so sor rnam par rig pa ni rnam par shes pa'o|| rnam par shes pa dang lhan cig byung ba nye bar len pa'i phung po bzhi po 'di dag ni ming dang gzugs so|| ming dang gzugs la rten pa'i dbang po rnams ni skye mched drug go|| chos gsum 'dus pa ni reg pa'o|| reg pa myong ba ni

tshor ba'o| tshor ba la zhen pa ni sred pa'o|| sred pa 'phel ba ni len pa'o|| len pa las skyes pa yang skyed pa'i las ni srid pa'o|| rgyu de las phung po byung ba ni skye ba'o|| skyes nas phung po smin pa ni rga ba'o|| rgas nas phung po zhig pa ni 'chi ba'o| 'chi zhing myos te mngon par chags pa dang bcas pa'i nang gi yongs su gdung ba ni mya ngan to|| mya ngan las byung ba'i tshig tu smra ba ni smre sngags 'don pa'o|| rnam par shes pa lnga'i tshogs dang ldan pa'i mi bde ba myong ba ni sdug bsngal lo|| yid la byed pa dang ldan pa'i yid kyi sdug bsngal ni yid mi bde ba'o|| gzhan yang 'di lta bu la sogs pa'i nye ba'i nyon mongs pa gang yin pa de dag ni 'khrug pa zhes bya'o||

Para. 27:
(1) For para. 2.7, C: What is ignorance? Ignorance produces out of the six factors the notion of one, a combination, eternality, constancy, indestructibility, inner happiness, (one of the) many beings, a life, a person, the notion of I and of mine. These manifold thoughts which arise in this way are known as ignorance. Thus greed and hatred are produced in the five senses, and thus there are perceptions and thought formations. All the deceptive mental phenomena following upon these are called consciousness. Four aggregates are name. The form aggregate is form. This is called name-and-form. The growth of name-and-form produces the six (sense) entrances. The growth of the six (sense) entrances produces contact ... sensation ... desire ... grasping ... becoming. And thus the growth of becoming can produce the subsequent aggregates, (which) is birth. The growth and transformation of birth is called old age. When the aggregates perish, it is called death. (This process) can produce a fever, (and is) therefore called grief, lamentation, suffering and depression. The five senses in contact with unpleasantness are called bodily suffering. An unharmonious mind is called mental suffering. (C. omits final sentence.) **(2)** *Ahaṁ-kāra* = "ego", the principle which, according to Sāṁkhya, develops the notion of self from the impersonal evolution of *prakṛti*. **(3)** The three "roots of unwholesomeness" (*akusala-mūlāni*). **(4)** *Viṣaya* = lit. "province, region", hence "sphere of activity (of the senses)", hence "sense object". **(5)** *Vastu-prativijñaptir*, but see Stcherbatsky, *Buddhist Logic II*, p. 173, n. 4: "mere sensation of something indefinite in the ken of our sense-faculties". **(6)** i.e. the conjunction of eye, visible object and visual consciousness, etc. Cp. M1:111; D2:62 and PTS transl. p. 59, n. 3. **(7)** Cp. S2:3 where *antaradhānam* = "disappearance" occurs instead of *antardāhaḥ* = "internal burning". **(8)** See para. 24 n. 3. **(9)** Ss., Msl., T: *manisikāra* = "attentiveness". instead of "the mind". **(10)** *Upakleśa*. Cp. the 16 *upakkilesa at M1:36 and the 10 kilesa* at *Dhs.* 1229. **(11-11)** Ss: *yā eṣv-eva ṣaṭsu dhātuṣv-ekasaṁjñā*. Bp: *eteṣām eva ṣaṇṇāṁ dhātūnāṁ yaikasaṁjñā*. Msl: *ya eṣv-eva saḍdhātuṣu ekasaṁjñā*. B: *tatraiteṣv-eva ṣaṭsu dhātuṣu yaikasaṁjñā*. **(12-12)** B. omits. **(13-13)** Mp. omits *ātmasaṁjñā*. Ss: *ātmasaṁjñā sattvajīvamanujamānavasaṁjñā*. Bp. *ātmasaṁjñā sattvasaṁjñā jīva° jantu° manuja° mānavasaṁjñā*. Msl: *sattvajīvajantupoṣapuruṣapudgalmanujamānavasaṁjñā*. T: *ātmasaṁjñā sattvajīvajantupoṣapuruṣapudgalasaṁjñā manujamānavasaṁjñā* (VP). B: *sattvasaṁjñā pudgalasaṁjñā manuṣyasaṁjñā mātṛduhitṛsaṁjñā*. **(14-14)** Ss: *°vividhajñānam°*. B: *so-amavi-dyā-saṁsārānarthasambhārasya mūlakāraṇaṁ*. **(15)** Ss., Msl: *amī ucyante saṁskārā iti*|. Bp., T: *amī avidyāpratyayāḥ saṁskārā ity-ucyante*|. B. *tasyām-avidyāyāṁ satyām saṁskārā rāgadveṣamohā viṣayeṣu pravartante*. **(16)** Msl: *vastuprajñaptiḥ indriyavijñānacetanā vijñānam*|. B: *vastuviṣayā vijñaptir-vijñānaṁ* **(17)** Following Ss. Mp: *vijñānasahabhuvaś-catvāraḥ skandhā arūpina upādānākhyāst-annāma rūpaṁ catvāri mahābhūtāni tāni copādāya rūpaṁ, tac-ca nāma ekadhyam-abhisaṁkṣipya tan nāmarūpaṁ*|.

Bp: catvāri mahābhūtani copādānāni rūpam-aikadhyarūpam| vijñāna sahajaś-çatvāro'rupiṇa upādānaskandhā nāma| 'tan nāmarūpaṁ|. Msl. (oddly, agreeing with T.): *vijñānasahajāś-catvāra upādānaskandhaḥ, tan nāmarūpam|*. B: *vijñānāccatvāro rūpiṇa* [sic] *upādāna skandhās-tan-nāma tāny-upādāyarūpam-abhinirvartate tad-aikadhyam-abhisaṁkṣipya nāmarūpaṁ niruchyate.* **(18)** Msl: *°saṁsritānīndriyāni...* Bp: *°saṁnisṛtāni...* B: śarīrasyaiva kalalabudbudādyavasthā, nāmarūpasaṁmiśritānīdriyāṇi ṣaḍāyatanaṁ. **(19)** Msl. adds: *viṣayendriyavijñānasaṁnipata ity-arthaḥ|*. B: *nāmarūpendriyāṇāṁ trayāṇāṁ sannipātaḥ sparśaḥ.* **(20)** Ss: *°anubhavanā.* B: *sparśād-vedanā sukhādikā.* **(21)** Msl. adds: *adhyavasānaṁ kāṅkśā sukhādhy-anubhavaḥ|*. B: *vedanāyāṁ satyāṁ kartavyam-etat-sukhaṁ punarmayetyadhyavasānaṁ tṛṣṇā bhavati.* **(22)** B: *tata upādānaṁ vākkāyaceṣṭā bhavati.* **(23)** B: *tato bhavaḥ bhavaty-asmāj-janmeti bhavo dharmādharmau.* **(24)** Ss., B., T: *taddhetuka* **(25)** B. adds: *janma.* **(26)** Bp: *jatyabhinirvṛttānāṁ skandhānāṁ pari°*. Ss: *|skandhapari°*. T: *jātaskandhaparipāko jarā|*. Msl: *skandaparipāko jarā skandhajirṇatety-arthaḥ|*. B: *janmahetukā uttare jarāmaraṇādayaḥ| jātānām skandhānāṁ paripako jarā.* **(27)** Ss: *|vinaśo maraṇaṁ|*. Bp., Msl: *|skandhavi°*. B:*skandhānāṁ nāśo°*. **(28)** Ss., Msl., B. omit *saṁ-*. **(29)** Ss: *svābhi°*. B: *°ṣvaṅgasya putrakalatrādāv-antardāhaḥ śokaḥ|*. **(30)** Ss: *lālapyanaṁparidevah* Bp., Msl: *śokenālapanaṁparidevanaṁ.* B: *taduttham pralapanaṁ hā mātaḥ hā tāta hā ca me putrakalatrādīti parideveṇa.* **(31)** Ss: *°saṁprayuktam-asātānu°*. Msl: *cakṣurādi-pañca°* ... *asātānuśayanaṁ duḥkhapaścattāpaṁ (duḥkha)|*. B: *°yuktam-asādhv-anu°* **(32)** Ss., Msl: *manasikārasaṁprayuktaṁ.* Bp: *duḥkhamanasikārasaṁprayuktaṁ.* T: *manasikārayuktaṁ.* B. omits phrase. **(33)** B. inserts: *ca.* **(34)** Ss., Bp., Msl: *ye cānye.* **(35)** Msl. inserts: *kleśāḥ.* **(36)** Bp: *°kleśā ima upāyāsā ity-ucyante|* Ss: *°kleśāsta upāyāsāḥ|| pe ||* Msl: *upakleśā upayāsāḥ manovikalpajātamāyāśāṭhyadainyakāmarāgādayas-te-sarve| peyālaṁ||* B: *evaṁ-jātīyakāś-copāyāsta upakleśā gṛhyante.* B. ends citation here.

Pāli: *katamañca bhikkhave nāmarūpaṁ. vedanā saññā cetanā phasso manasikāro, idaṁ vuccati nāmaṁ. cattāro ca mahābhūtā catunnañca mahābhūtānaṁ upādāya rūpaṁ, idaṁ vuccati rūpaṁ. iti idañca nāmaṁ idañca rūpaṁ, idaṁ vuccati bhikkhave nāmarūpam* (S2:3-4). *cakkhuñcāvuso paṭicca rūpe ca uppajjati cakkhuviññāṇaṁ, tiṇṇaṁ saṅgati phasso, phassapaccayā vedanā, yaṁ vedeti taṁ sañjānāti, yaṁ sañjānāti taṁ vitakketi, yaṁ vitakketi taṁ papañceti ...* (M1:111-12). *indriyānaṁ paripāko, ayaṁ vuccati jarā. yaṁ tesaṁ tesaṁ sattānaṁ tamhā tamhā sattanikāyā cuticavanatā bhedo antardhānaṁ ... idaṁ vuccati maraṇaṁ. ... khandhānaṁ pātubhāvo āyatanāṁ paṭilābho, ayaṁ vuccati bhikkhave jāti* (S2:3).

SF: ... *(ga)ng gcig pur 'du shes pa| ril por 'du shes (pa da)ng rtag par 'du shes pa| brtan bar 'du shes pa| ther zug du 'du shes pa| bde bar 'du shes pa| sems can dang srog dang skye ba dang gso' ba dang skyes (bu) ... (shed bu) du 'du shes pa dang| nga zhes bya ba dang bdagi zhes bya bar 'du shes pa 'di lta bu las stsogs pa myi shes pa rnam pa sna tshogs pa 'di lta bu ni ma rig pa zhes bya'o| de ltar ma rig pa yod pas yul (r)na(ms la ')dod chags ... 'jug go| de la yul rnams la 'dod chags dang zhe sdang dang gti mug pa gang yin ba 'di ni 'du byed rnams so dngos po so sor rnam par rig pa rnam par shes pa'o| rnam par shes pa dang lhan chig (sky)e (ba nye bar len pa'i) phung po gzugs myed pa bzhi po de dag ni mying dang gzugs so| mying dang gzugs la rten pa'i dbang po rnams ni skye mched drug go| chos gsum 'dus pa ni reg pa'o| reg pa myong ba ni tshor ba'o| tshor ba las zhen (ba ni sred pa'o| sred pa) 'pheld pa ni lend pa'o| len pha las skyes pa yang srid pa skyed pa'i las ni srid pa'o| rgyu de las phung po byung ba ni skye ba'o| skyes nas phung po smyind pa ni rgas pa'o (||) rgas nas phung po ... myi bde ba myong ba ni sdu(g bsngal lo||)*

28.[1] (It is called) ignorance in the sense of making a great blindness, (mental) formations in the sense of formation, consciousness in the sense of causing to know, name-and-form in the sense of mutual support, six (sense) entrances in the sense of entrance doors, (sensual) contact in the sense of contacting, feelings in the sense of experiencing, desire in the sense of thirsting, grasping in the sense of grasping, becoming in the sense of giving birth to repeated becoming, birth in the sense of manifestation of the aggregates, decay in the sense of maturing of the aggregates, death in the sense of perishing, grief in the sense of grieving, lamentation in the sense of verbal lamentation, suffering in the sense of bodily torment, depression in the sense of mental torment, anxiety in the sense of subtle defilement.

Bp. 388 Mp. 564
28.[2] tatra mahāndhakārārthenāvidyā,[3] abhisaṁskārārthena saṁskārāh, vijñāpanārthena vijñānaṁ, anyo 'nyopastambhanārthena[4] nāmarūpaṁ, āyadvārārthena ṣaḍ-āyatanaṁ, sparśanārthena sparśaḥ, anubhavanārthena vedanā, paritarṣaṇārthena tṛṣṇā, upādānārthenopādānaṁ, punarbhavajanārthena[5] bhavaḥ, skandhaprādurbhāvārthena[6] jātiḥ, skandhaparipākārthena[7] jarā, vināśārthena maraṇaṁ, śocanārthena śokaḥ, vacanaparidevanārthena[8] paridevaḥ, kāyasaṁpīḍanārthena[9] duḥkhaṁ, cittasaṁpīḍanārthena daurmanasyaṁ, upakleśanārthenopāyāsāḥ||[10]

28. de la mun pa chen po'i phyir ma rig pa'o|| mngon par 'du byed pa'i phyir 'du byed rnams so|| rnam par rig pa'i phyir rnam par shes pa'o|| rten pa'i phyir ming dang gzugs so|| skye ba'i sgo'i phyir skye mched drug go|| reg pa'i phyir reg pa'o|| myong ba'i phyir tshor ba'o|| skom pa'i phyir sred pa'o|| nye bar len pa'i phyir len pa'o|| yang srid pa skye ba'i phyir srid pa'o|| phung po 'byung ba'i phyir skye ba'o|| phung po smin pa'i phyir rga ba'o|| 'jig pa'i phyir 'chi ba'o|| mya ngan byed pa'i phyir mya ngan to|| tshig gis smre ba'i phyir smre sngags 'don pa'o|| lus la gnod pa'i phyir sdug bsngal pa'o || sems la gnod pa'i phyir yid mi bde ba'o|| nyon mongs pa'i phyir 'khrug pa'o||

(1) For para. 28, C: Thus these many sufferings together, always in darkness, are called ignorance. (Mental) construction and all actions (karma) are called (mental) formations. (That which) discriminates all *dharmas* is called consciousness. (That which) is established is called name-and-form. The (sense) bases opening up are called the six entrances. (If there is) the meeting of (these) conditions, worldly objects are apprehended; therefore it is called contact. Sensations feel suffering and joy; therefore (they are) called sensations. (It is) like thirsting for a drink, therefore (it is) called desire. There can be grasping; therefore it is called grasping. It creates all actions (karma); therefore (it is) called becoming. The aggregates appear; therefore it is called birth. Living in the world and becoming weak is called old age. Finally perishing is called death. Regretting past events and giving vent to sadness is called lamentation. Things which torment the body are called suffering. Recalling (these) together is called grief. Bondage to worries is called anxiety. (2) Ss., Msl. omit para. 28. Bp. and T. agree on several readings in para. 28 which seem better than Mp. (3) Mp: *mohāndha°*. (4) Bp: *mana-*

nārthena. (5) Mp: *punarbhavārthena*. Cp. para. 27. (6) Mp: *(bhavaḥ,) janmanārthena* ... Cp. para. 27. (7) Mp. omits *skandha*. (8) Mp. omits *vacana*. (9) Mp: *kāyaparipf132(dana°*, but *saṁpīdana* in next phrase. T: *pīdanārthena*. (10) Bp. 389 ends citation with: *iti vistaraḥ||*

Pāli: *indriyānaṁ paripāko, ayaṁ vuccati jarā. ... khandhānaṁ pātubhāvo ... ayaṁ vuccati bhikkhave jāti* (S2:3, cp. para. 27).

SF: ... *mngon bar 'du byed (pa'i phyir) ... skom ba'i phyir sred (pa'o||) ... smre sngags 'dond (pa'o||)...*

29.[1] Otherwise, not arriving at reality, arriving at falsehood, misapprehension is ignorance. Thus, when there is ignorance, the three-fold (mental) formations develop: leading to advantage leading to disadvantage, and leading to stability.[2] (As a result) of the (mental) formations leading to advantage, advantageous consciousness occurs. (As a result) of the (mental) formations leading to disadvantage, disadvantageous consciousness occurs. (As a result) of the (mental) formations leading to stability, stable consciousness occurs. This is called consciousness conditioned by (mental) formations. As for consciousness-conditioned name-and-form, the four non-material aggregates, sensations etc., cause bending[3] into existence here and there, and so are called name. (This) name, which accompanies form, plus form (itself) is called name-and-form. By the growth of name-and-form, through the six (sense) entrance doors, activities develop. This is called, the six (sense) entrances conditioned by name-and-form. Because of the six (sense) entrances, the six contact bodies[4] develop. This is called contact conditioned by the six (sense) entrances. Whatever type of contact occurs, that type of sensation develops. This is called sensation conditioned by contact. That which, by discriminating those sensations, causes one to relish, that which delights, clings, and clinging remains, that is called desire conditioned by sensations. (Thus) relishing, delighting and clinging, there is non-renunciation, the repeated wish: "May these dear forms, delightful forms[5] not be separated from me". This is called grasping conditioned by desire. This wishing causes rebirth-producing *karma* to arise by means of body, speech and mind. This is called becoming conditioned by grasping. The development of the aggregates born (as a result) of that *karma* is called birth conditioned by becoming. Due to increase and maturity, the perishing of the aggregates developed by birth occurs. This is called decay and death conditioned by birth.

Mp. 564 Ss. 223 Bp. 479 Msl. 111

29. atha-vā[6] tattve 'pratipattir-mithyāpratipattir-ājñānam-avidyā||[7] evam-avidyāyāṁ[8] satyāṁ trividāḥ saṁskārā abhinirvartante, puṇyopagā apuṇyopagā [9]āneñjyopagāḥ|| tatra[9] puṇyopagānāṁ saṁskārāṇāṁ puṇyopagam-eva vijñānaṁ bhavati| apuṇyopagānāṁ saṁskārāṇām-apuṇyopagam-eva vijñānaṁ bhavati| āneñjyopagānāṁ saṁskārāṇām-āneñjyopagam-eva[10] vijñānaṁ bhavati| idam-ucyate saṁskārapratyayaṁ vijñānam-iti|[11] [12]vijñānapratyayaṁ nāmarūpam-iti vedanādayo 'rūpiṇaś-catvāraḥ skandhās-tatra tatra bhave nāmayantīti nāma| saharūpaskandhena ca nāma rūpaṁ ceti nāmarūpam-ucyate||[12] nāmarūpavivṛddhyā ṣaḍbhir-āyatanadvāraiḥ kṛtyakriyāḥ pravartante[13]| tan nāmarūpapratyayaṁ ṣaḍ-āyatānām-ity-ucyate[14]| ṣaḍbhyaś-cāyatanebhyaḥ[15] ṣaṭ sparśakāyāḥ[16] pravartante| ayaṁ ṣaḍ-āyatanapratyayaḥ sparśa

ity-ucyate[17]|| yaj-jātīyaḥ sparśo bhavati taj-jātīyā vedanā pravartante[18]| iyam sparśapratyayā vedanety-ucyate||[19] yas-taṁ vedanāṁ[20] viśeṣeṇāsvādayati abhinandati[21] [22]adhyavasyati adhyavasāya tiṣṭhati,[22] sā vedanāpratyayā tṛṣṇety-ucyate|| [23]āsvādanābhinandanādhyavasānaṁ| mā me priyarūpaśātarūpairviyogo bhavatv-iti, aparityāgo bhūyo bhūyaś-ca prārthanā| idam tṛṣṇāpratyayam-upādānām-ity-ucyate|[23] [24] evaṁ prārthayamānaḥ punar-bhavajanakaṁ karma samutthāpayati kāyena vācā manasā[25] ca[26]| sa[27] upādānapratyayo bhava ity-ucyate|| tatkarmanirjātānāṁ[28] skandhānām-abhinirvṛttir-yā[29] sā bhavapratyayā jātir-ity-ucyate|| [30] jātyābhinirvṛttānāṁ skandānām-upacayanaparipākād-vināśo[31] bhavati| tad-idaṁ jātipratyayaṁ jarāmaraṇam-ity-ucyate[32]||

29. gzhan yang de kho na mi rtogs shing log par shes te mi shes pa ni ma rig pa'o|| de ltar ma rig pa yod na 'du byed rnam gsum mngon par 'grub ste| bsod nams su nye bar 'gro ba dang| bsod nams ma yin par nye bar 'gro ba dang| mi g.yo bar nye bar 'gro ba'o|| de la bsod nams su nye bar 'gro ba'i 'du byed rnams las bsod nams su nye bar 'gro ba'i rnam par shes pa nyid du 'gyur ba dang| bsod nams ma yin par nye bar 'gro ba'i 'du byed rnams las bsod nams ma yin par nye bar 'gro ba'i rnam par shes pa nyid du 'gyur ba dang| mi g.yo bar nye bar 'gro ba'i 'du byed rnams las mi g.yo bar nye bar 'gro ba'i rnam par shes pa nyid du 'gyur ba 'di ni 'du byed kyi rkyen gyis rnam par shes pa zhes bya'o|| rnam par shes pa dang lhan cig skyes pa phung po gzugs can ma yin pa bzhi dang| gzugs gang yin pa de ni rnam par shes pa'i rkyen gyis ming dang gzugs shes bya'o|| ming dang gzugs rnam par 'phel bas skye mched drug gi sgo nas bya ba byed pa rnams 'byung ste| de ni ming dang gzugs kyi rkyen gyis skye mched drug ces bya'o| skye mched drug po dag la reg pa'i tshogs drug 'byung ste| 'di ni skye mched drug gi rkyen gyis reg pa zhes bya'o|| ji lta bur reg pa 'byung ba de lta bu tshor ba 'byung ste| de ni reg pa'i rkyen gyis tshor ba zhes bya'o|| tshor ba'i bye brag de dag myong ba dang| mngon par dga' ba dang| lhag par zhen pa dang| lhag par zhen nas 'dug pa de ni tshor ba'i rkyen gyis sred pa zhes bya'o|| myong ba dang| mngon par dga' ba dang| lhag par zhen pa dang| lhag par zhen nas 'dug pa las bdag sdug pa'i ngo bo dang| bde ba'i ngo bo dang 'bral bar ma gyur cig snyam du yongs su mi gtong bar phyir zhing smon pa 'di ni sred pa'i rkyen gyis len pa zhes bya'o|| de ltar smon zhing yang srid pa bskyed pa'i las| lus dang| ngag dang yid kyis kun nas slong ba de ni len pa'i rkyen gyis srid pa zhes bya'o|| las de las skyes pa'i phung po lnga rnams 'grub pa gang yin pa de ni srid pa'i rkyen gyis skye ba zhes bya'o|| skye nas mngon du 'grub pa'i phung po rnams kyi 'phel ba yongs su smin pa dang| 'jig par 'gyur ba de ni skye ba'i rkyen gyis rga shi zhes bya'o||

(1) For para. 29, C: Pernicious views and confused understandings are called ignorance. These pernicious (views and confused) understandings produce the three (types of) action (*karma*), which are therefore called (mental) activities. Good and bad actions can yield results, which are therefore called consciousness. From defiled, unmindful actions, defiled unmindful conscious-

ness is born. From stable actions, stable consciousness is born. Consciousness produces name and form ... (etc., repeating the bare *pratītyasamutpāda* formula). **(2)** Cp. the three *abhisankhāras* at Vbh. 135. On *anañja*° see Vsm. 386. **(3)** "Cause bending" = *nāmayanti*, a pseudo-etymological definition based on a pun as at Vsm. 558. **(4)** *sparśakāya*, the six types of sensual contact, visual etc., involving organ, object and consciousness. See para. 24, n. 3, para. 27, n. 6. **(5)** Cp. Pali *piyarūpaṁ sātarūpaṁ* at S2:109 etc. **(6)** Ss., Bp., Msl: *punar-aparaṁ*. **(7)** Bp. also quotes first sentence on p. 352. Msl: °*ajñānam saṁvṛtiparamārthayor-vibhāgajñanam ajñanam*| **(8)** Msl. omits *evam*. **(9-9)** Ss: °*opagaś-cema ucyante 'vidyāpratyayāḥ saṁskārā iti*| (*puny*°). Bp: as Ss., but: *anaṁjyopagāś-ca*| Msl: *aniñjyopagaś-ceti saṁbhāvante avidyāpratyayāḥ saṁskārā iti*|. **(10)** Bp: *anaṁjyopagānam ... anaṁjyopagam-eva*. **(11)** Mp: *idam-ucyate (vijñānapratyayaṁ)*, an omission. **(12-12)** Ss: *evaṁ nāmarūpam*| Bp., Msl: *tad-eva vijñānapratyayaṁ nāmarūpam*| T: *vijñānasahajāś-catvaro'rūpiṇaḥ skandhā yac-ca rūpaṁ tad-eva vijñānapratyayaṁ nāmarūpam ity-ucyate* (VP). **(13)** Msl. adds: *prajñāyante*. **(14)** Bp., Msl. omit *iti*. **(15)** Ss., Bp., Msl. omit *ca*. **(16)** Msl: °*kāyasamūhāḥ*. **(17)** Msl. omits *iti*. **(18)** Ss. and Msl: *pravartate*. **(19)** Msl: ... *vedanā ucyate*|| Mp: *iyam ucyate bhikṣavaḥ sparśapratyayā vedaneti*|| **(20)** Ss., Bp., Msl: *vedayati*. **(21)** Bp. °*nandayati*. **(22-22)** Ss., Bp: *adhyavasyaty-adhitiṣ*°. Msl: *adhyavasati kāṅkṣati adhitiṣ*°. **(23-23)** Mp: °*dhyavasānasthānād-ātmapriyarūpasātarūpair-viyogo mā bhūn-nityam-aparityāgo bhaved iti prārthanā ida-mucyate bhikṣavas-tṛṣṇapratyayam-upādānam*| Bp: °*dhyāvasāyasthānaṁ ātmapriyasātarūpair-viyogo mā bhavatv-iti* ... Msl: °*dhyavasāyasthānam na me priyarūpasātarūpaiḥ pañcabhiḥ kāmagunair-viyogo bhavatu aparityāgaḥ* ... T: °*nandanādhyavasānādhyavasāyasthānād ātmapriyarūpasātarūpair viyogo ma bhavatv-iti aparityagād prārthanā idam* ... **(24)** Mp. inserts: *yatra vastuni satṛṣṇastasya vastuno'rjanāya viṭhapanāyopādānam-upadatte tatra tatra prārthayate, (evaṁ ...)*. **(25)** Msl: *kāyena manasā vācā*| (*sa* ...). **(26)** Ss., Bp., Msl. omit *ca*. **(27)** Ss: *ayam*. **(28)** Ss: *yā karmanirjātā*. Msl. *yat karma*°. **(29)** Ss., Msl. omit *ya*. T: *pañcaskandhānam*°. **(30)** Ss., Msl. insert *yo*. Bp. inserts *yā*. **(31)** Ss., Msl: °*upacayapari*°. Bp. °*upapari*°. **(32)** Ss. omits *iti*.

Pāli: *yaṁ kho bhikkhave dukkhe ... dukkhasamudaye ... dukkhanirodhe ... paṭipadāya aññāṇaṁ, ayaṁ vuccati bhikkhave avijjā* (S2:4). *vedanā saññā cetanā phasso manasikāro, idaṁ vuccati nāmaṁ. cattāro ca mahābhūtā catunnañca mahābhūtānaṁ upādāya rūpaṁ, idaṁ vuccati rūpaṁ. iti idañca nāmaṁ idañca rūpaṁ, idaṁ vuccati bhikkhave nāmarūpaṁ* (S2:3-4, cp. para. 27) *rūpaṁ ... vedanaṁ ... saññaṁ ... sankhāre ... viññāṇaṁ abhinandato abhivadato ajjhosāya tiṭṭhato uppajati nandi. yā viññāṇe nandi tadupādānaṁ* (S3:14).

SF: ... *de ltar ma rig pa yod na 'du byed rnam gsum mngon bar 'gru(b ste)*| *bsod namsu nye bar 'gro ba dang*| *bsod (nams ma yin bar) nye bar 'gro ba dang*| *myi gyo bar nye bar 'gro ba'o*| *de la bsod na(ms) ... nams su nye bar 'gro ba'i rnam par shes pa nyid du 'gyur ba dang*| *b(sod) nams ma yin bar nye bar 'gro (ba'i 'du byed rnam)s las bsod nams ma yin bar nye bar 'gro ba'i rnam (par shes pa ... nye) bar 'gro ba'i 'du byed rnams las myi g.yo bar nye bar 'gro ba'i (rnam) par shes pa nyid du 'gyur ba '(di ni 'du byed kyi) rky(e)nd kyis rnam par shes pa zhes bya'o*| *de bzhin du rnam pa(r shes pa'i) ... mying dang gzugs rnam par 'pheld pas skye mched drug gi sgo nas bya ba byed pa rnams 'byung ste '(di) n(i) myi(ng dang gzugs ky)i (rky)e(nd ky)i(s) skye mched drug ces bya'o*| *skye mched drug ... skye mched drug gi rkyend kyis reg pa zhes bya'o*| *ji lta bur reg pa 'byung ba de lta bur tshor myong ste de ni reg pa'i rkyend kyis tshor ba'i (by)e brag de dag myong ba dang ... (yid kyis kun nas slong) ba de ni (len pa'i ... 'grug pa gang) yin (pa ... 'phel ba yongs) su zug(s pa dang*| *'jig par 'gyur ...)*.

30.[1] Thus, this twelve-fold conditioned arising with interdependence of causes and interdependence of conditions, not impermanent, not permanent, not compounded, not uncompounded, not without cause, not without condition not an experiencer, not a destructable thing, not a ceasing thing, not a perishable thing, not proceeding from premordial time, not cut off, rolls along like a flowing stream.[2]

Mp. 566

30.[3] evam-ayaṁ dvādaśāṅgaḥ pratītyasamutpādo 'nyonyahetuko-'nyonyapratyayo-naivānityo na nityo[4] na saṁskṛto nāsaṁskṛto nāhetuko nāpratyayo[5] na vedayitā [6] na kṣayadharmo [7] na vināśadharmo [8] na nirodhadharmo [9] 'nādikālapravṛtto 'nucchinno 'nupravartate nadisrotavat||

30. de ltar rten cing 'brel bar 'byung ba'i yan lag bcu gnyis po 'di dag ni [10]rgyu gzhan dang gzhan las byung ba| rkyen gzhan dang gzhan las byung ba|[10] rtag pa ma yin| mi rtag pa ma yin| 'dus byas ma yin| 'dus ma byas ma yin| rgyu med pa ma yin| rkyen med pa ma yin| myong ba yod pa ma yin| zad pa'i chos ma yin| 'jig pa'i chos ma yin| 'gog pa'i chos ma yin te| thog ma med pa'i dus nas[11] zhugs pa| rgyun ma chad par klung[12] gi rgyun bzhin du[13] rjes su zhugs pa'o[14]||

(1) Inexplicably, Ss., Bp. and Msl. all omit paras. 30-31, leaving only Mp., T., and SF as sources, as well as, oddly, the Tibetan Ss., which, like SF, consolidates paras. 30 and 31 by omitting the extensive repetition in T. and the repeated phrase (not cut off ... stream) in Mp. In true Madhyamaka style, Mp. follows each of the denied attributes in these paras. with a denial of the opposite attribute as well. The Tibetan sources do not, so Mp. appears to be a distortion. Therefore, paras. 30-31 follow T. for content and Mp. for precise terminology. Minor variations between T. and TSs. are noted for these paras. **(2)** For para. 30, C. has: Maitreya said to Venerable Śāriputra, "Each of the twelve causes and conditions has a result. (It is) not eternal, not annihilated, not active, not inactive, not a perishable thing (*fa=dharma*), not free of desire, not a destructible thing. Whether there is a Buddha or not, the succession is unbroken. Like a stream it flows for limitless time." **(3)** Ss: *pe.* Bp: *peyālam.* Msl: *peyālam, tatra avidyādiṣu śokaparideva-duḥkhadaurmanasyopāyāsāḥ peyalārthena nidarśitāḥ|* Each omits paras. 30-31. See n. 1. **(4)** T: *na nityo nānityo.* **(5)** Mp. omits. **(6)** Mp. inserts: *nāvedayitā na pratītyasamutpanno nāpratītyasamutpanno.* **(7)** Mp. inserts: *nākṣayadharmo.* **(8)** Mp. inserts: *nāvināśadharmo.* **(9)** Mp. inserts: *nānirodhadharmo.* **(10-10)** TSs: *gcig gi rgyu gcig gcig gi rkyen cig|.* Cp. SF, para. 31. **(11)** TSs: *na.* **(12)** P. and TSs: *rlung.* **(13)** TSs. omits. **(14)** TSs: *mod kyi* (omitting repetition of para. 30 in para. 31, and thereby skipping to para. 31: *hon kyang yan lag bzhi po ...*; see n.1)

SF: See para. 31, SF, and para. 30, n. 1.

31.[1] As this conditioned arising, not cut off, rolls along like a flowing stream, four limbs of this twelve-fold conditioned arising develop through (the process of) causality for (performing) the action of assembling. What four? Namely: ignorance, desire, karma and consciousness.[2]

Mp. 566
31.[3] [4]yady-apy-ayaṁ [5] pratītyasamutpādo 'nucchino 'nupravartate nadisrotavat,[4] atha cemāny-asya dvādaśāṅgasya pratītyasamutpādasya catvāry-aṅgāni saṁghātakriyāyai hetutvena pravartante| katamāni catvāri| yadutāvidyā tṛṣṇā karma vijñānaṁ ca|

31. [6]rten cing 'brel bar 'byung ba'i yan lag bcu gnyis po 'di dag ni rgyu gzhan dang gzhan las byung ba| rkyen gzhan dang gzhan las byung ba| rtag pa ma yin| mi rtag pa ma yin| 'dus byas ma yin| 'dus ma byas ma yin| rgyu med pa ma yin| rkyen med pa ma yin| myong ba yod pa ma yin| zad pa'i chos ma yin| 'jig pa'i chos ma yin| 'gog pa'i chos ma yin te| thog ma med pa'i dus nas zhugs pa rgyun ma chad par klung gi rgyun bzhin du rjes su zhugs mod kyi|[6] 'on kyang yan lag bzhi po 'di dag ni rten cing 'brel bar 'byung ba'i yan lag bcu gnyis po de dag bsdu bar bya ba'i rgyu'i 'gyur ro|| bzhi gang zhe na| 'di lta ste| ma rig pa dang| sred pa dang| las dang| rnam par shes pa'o||

(1) See para. 30, n. 1. **(2)** For para. 31, C. repeats para. 30 and adds: The twelve conditions can increase with four conditions. What four? Ignorance, desire, karma, and consciousness. **(3)** Ss., Bp, Msl. omit para. 31. See para. 30, n. 1, 3 and 14. **(4-4)** T. repeats para. 30: *dvādaśāṅgaḥ ... nadisrotavat|* (*atha ...*). **(5)** T. inserts: *dvādaśāṅgaḥ*. **(6-6)** TSs. omits. See para. 30, n. 1 and 14, and re-apply variations in para. 30, n. 10 and 11.

SF: (*gcig gi rgyu gcig gi*) *rkyend gcig| rtag pa ma yin myi rtag pa ma yin| 'dus byas ma yin 'dus ma byas ma yin| myong ... rky(e)nd myed pa las byung ba ma yin| zad pa'i chos ma yin| 'jig pa'i chos ma yin| 'gog pa' chos ma yin te thog ma myed pa'i dus nas klung gi rgyun bzhin du ma chad par zhugs pa'i rjesu zhugs mo(d kyi| hon kyang yan lag bzhi) po 'di dag ni de bsdu bar bya ba'i rgyur 'gro'o| bzhi gang zhe na 'di lta ste| ma rig pa dang| sred pa dang| las dang rnam par shes pa'o|*

32. Therein, consciousness is a cause by being of the nature of a seed. Karma is a cause by being of the nature of a field. Ignorance and desire are a cause by being of the nature of defilement. Karma-defilements cause the consciousness-seed to be born. Therein, karma performs the function of being the field of the consciousness-seed. Desire waters the consciousness-seed. Ignorance scatters the consciousness-seed. Without these conditions, the development of the consciousness-seed does not occur.[1]

Mp. 566 Ss. 224 Bp. 480 Msl. 112
32. tatra vijñānaṁ bījasvabhāvatvena hetuḥ| karma kṣetrasvabhāvatvena hetuḥ| avidyā tṛṣṇā ca kleśasvabhāvatvena hetuḥ|

karmakleśā vijñānabījaṁ janayanti[2]| tatra karma vijñānabījasya kṣetrakāryaṁ karoti| tṛṣṇā vijñānabījaṁ snehayati| avidyā vijñānabījam-avakirati| asatāṁ teṣāṁ pratyayānāṁ vijñānabījasyābhinirvṛttir-na [3] bhavati|[4]

32. de la rnam par shes pa ni sa bon gyis rang bzhin gyis rgyu byed do|| las ni zhing gi rang bzhin gyis rgyu byed do|| ma rig pa dang sred pa ni nyon mongs pa'i rang bzhin gyis rgyu byed do|| de la las dang nyon mongs pa dag ni sa bon rnam par shes pa skyed do|| de la las ni sa bon rnam par shes pa'i zhing gi bya ba byed do|| sred pa ni sa bon rnam par shes pa rlan par byed do|| ma rig pa ni sa bon rnam par shes pa 'debs te| rkyen 'di dag med na sa bon rnam par shes pa mngon par 'grub par mi 'gyur ro||

(1) C. omits last sentence. (2) Ss., Bp: *saṁjanayanti*| (3) Mp. omits *vijñāna*. (4) Ss. omits. Bp., Msl: *satām-eṣam* ... °*nirvṛttir-bhavati*|

Pāli: *iti kho ānanda kammaṁ khettaṁ viññāṇaṁ bījaṁ taṇhā sineho avijjānīvaraṇānam sattānaṁ taṇhāsaṁyojanānaṁ hīnāya dhātuyā viññāṇaṁ patiṭṭhitaṁ* (A1:223).

SF: *de la rnam par shes pa ni sa bon gyi rang bzhin gyis rgyu byed do| la(s ni zhing gi rang) bzhin gyi(s rgyu byed do| ma ri)g pa dang sred pa ni nyon mongs pa'i rang bzhin gyis rgyu byed do| de la las dang nyon mongs pa dag ni sa bon rnam par shes pa skyed do| de la las ni sa bon rnam par shes pa'i zhing gi bya ba byed do| (sred pa ni sa bo)n rnam pa(r shes pa rlan bar bye)d do| ma rig pa ni sa bon rnam par shes pa 'debs te| rkyend 'di dag myed na sa bon rnam par shes pa mngon bar 'grub par myi 'gyur ro|*

33. Therein, it does not occur to karma, "I perform the function of being the field of the consciousness-seed."[1] It does not occur to desire, "I water the consciousness-seed." It does not occur to ignorance, "I scatter the consciousness-seed."[2] Nor does it occur to the consciousness-seed, "I am born by (way of) these conditions."[3]

Mp. 566 Ss. 224 Bp. 481 Msl. 112

33. tatra karmaṇo[4] naivaṁ bhavati, ahaṁ vijñānabījasya[5] kṣetrakāryaṁ karomīti| tṛṣṇāyā api naivaṁ bhavati, ahaṁ vijñānabījaṁ[6] snehayāmīti[7]| avidyāyā[8] api naivaṁ bhavati ahaṁ vijñānabījam-avakirāmīti| vijñānabījasyāpi naivaṁ bhavati, aham-ebhiḥ pratyayair-janitam-iti[9]||

33. de la las kyang 'di snyam du bdag gis sa bon rnam par shes pa'i zhing gi bya ba bya'o snyam du mi sems so|| sred pa yang 'di snyam du bdag gis sa bon rnam par shes pa brlan par bya'o snyam du mi sems so|| ma rig pa yang 'di snyam du bdag gis sa bon rnam par shes pa gdab bo snyam du mi sems so|| sa bon rnam par shes pa yang 'di snyam du bdag ni rkyen 'di dag gis bskyed do snyam du mi sems te|

(1) C: "... I can produce the consciousness seed". (2) C: "... I can plant ...". (3) C: "... causes and conditions". (4) Bp: °*ṇām*. (5) Bp. omits *bījasya*. (6) Mp: *vijñānasya bījasya*. (7) Mp: *snehakāryaṁ karomīti*|. (8) Bp: *avidyā*. (9) Ss. °*janita iti*||. Msl: ... *pratyayairpratītyotpādairjanita iti*||.

SF: *de la las kyang 'di ltar bdag gis sa bon rnam par shes pa'i zhing gi (bya ba bya'o snyam) du myi (s)e(ms so| sred pa yang ')di ltar bdag gis sa bon rnam par shes pa rlan bar bya'o snyam du myi semso| ma rig pa yang 'di ltar bdag gis sa bon rnam par shes pa gdab bo snyam du myi sems so| sa bon rnam par shes pa yang 'di ltar bdag ni rkyen 'di dag gis bskyed do snyam du myi sems te|*

34. [1]And so, the consciousness-seed grows, standing in the karma-field, watered by the moisture of desire, scattered by ignorance. Here and there in the entrances of arising, it causes the sprout of name-and-form to develop through rebirth in a mother's womb.[1] And this sprout of name-and-form is not self made, not made by another, not made by both, not made by God, not transformed by time, not derived from *prakṛti*, not founded upon a single principle,[2] yet not arisen without cause. And so from the union of the mother and father in the (fertile) period, and by the conjunction of other conditions, [3]the consciousness-seed, permeated by appetite, causes the sprout of name-and-form to develop in a mother's womb, in (relation to) things (which are) not governed, not "mine" not possessed, (not opposed,)* like space, of the nature of the marks of illusion,[4] due to the non-deficiency of causes and conditions.[3]

Mp. 567 Ss. 224 Bp. 481 Msl. 112

34. atha-ca[5] [6]vijñānabījaṁ karmakṣetrapratiṣṭhitaṁ tṛṣṇāsnehābhiṣyanditam-avidyāvakīrṇaṁ virohati,[6] [7]tatratatropapattyāyatanapratisaṁdhau mātuḥ kukṣau[7] nāmarūpāṅkuram-abhinirvartayati[8]| sa ca[9] nāmarūpāṅkuro na svayaṁkṛto na parakṛto nobhayakṛto neśvaranirmito[10] na kālapariṇāmito na prakṛtisambhūto[11] na caikakāraṇādhīno[12] nāpy-ahetu samutpannaḥ|| atha ca mātāpitṛsaṁyogāt, ṛtusamavāyāt, anyeṣāṁ ca[13] pratyayānaṁ samavāyāt, āsvādānu-viddhaṁ[14] vijñānabījaṁ [15] mātuḥ kukṣau nāmarūpāṅkuram-abhinirvartayati,[16] [17]asvāmikeṣu dharmeṣu amameṣu aparigraheṣu (apratyarthikeṣu) ākāśasameṣu[17] māyālakṣaṇasvabhāveṣu[18] hetupratyayānām-avaikalyāt|

34. 'on kyang sa bon rnam par shes pa las kyi zhing la brten pa| sred pa'i rlan gyis rlan pa| ma rig pa'i lud kyis bran pa| skye ba na skye ba'i gnas nyid mtshams sbyor ba| ma'i mngal de dang der ming dang gzugs kyi myu gu mngon par 'grub ste| ming dang gzugs kyi myu gu de yang bdag gis ma byas| gzhan gyis ma byas| gnyis kas ma byas| dbang phyug gis ma byas| dus kyis ma bsgyur|

rang bzhin las ma byung| byed pa la rag las pa ma yin| rgyu med pa las kyang mi skyes te| 'on kyang pha dang ma phrad pa dang| zla mtshan dang ldan pa dang| rkyen gzhan yang 'tshogs na bdag po med pa'i chos| bdag gi med pa| 'dsin pa med pa| nam mka' dang mtshungs pa| sgyu ma'i mtshan nyid kyi rang bzhin dag la rgyu dang rkyen ma tshang ba med pa'i phyir skye ba'i gnas nyid mtshams sbyor ba ma'i mngal de dang der myong ba dang ldan pa'i sa bon rnam par shes pa ming dang gzugs kyi myu gu mngon par 'grub bo||

(1-1) C: Once again, *karma* is the consciousness field. Ignorance is dung. Desire is the water for soaking. Therefore the sprouts of name-and-form, etc., are produced. **(2)** C. omits: not ... principle. **(3-3)** C: The sprout of name-and-form arises. (It is) not a master, not a self, not a creator, not a life, like empty space, like illusion, born from many causes and conditions together. **(4)** *Māyā-lakṣaṇa-svabhāva*, i.e. illusory. **(5)** Ss., Bp., Msl: *api tu.* **(6–6)** Following Bp. and Msl. Mp: *°avidyayā svavakirṇam vibhajyamānaṁ virohati.* Ss: *°bije ... ṣṭhite ...ṣyandite'vidyāvakīrṇe (tatra ...).* T: ... moistened by the manure of ignorance (!) **(7-7)** Bp., Msl. omit. Ss: *°tatra tatropatty āyatanasaṁdhau mātuḥ kukṣau virohati* | *(nāma°).* **(8)** Ss., Bp., Msl: *°āṅkurasyābhinirvṛttir-bhavati*| **(9)** Msl: *cāsau.* **(10)** Mp., T: *°kṛto.* SF: *spruld = nirmito.* Ss: *neśvarādi°.* **(11)** Ss., Bp. omit. **(12)** Msl: *nākāraṇādhīno.* **(13)** Mp. omits. **(14)** Ss: *°ānupraviddhaṁ.* Bp: *°ānuprabaddhaṁ.* Msl: *°āsvadātprabuddhaṁ* (!) **(15)** Bp., Msl. and T. insert: *tatra tatropapattyāyatanapratisaṁdhau.* **(16)** Ss: *°aṅkurabījam-abhinirvartati.* **(17-17)** Following Ss. Bp. as Ss., but observes *yan sandhi* and: *°ākāśaṣu...* T. omits *apratyarthikeṣu.* Mp: ... *dharmeṣv-aparigraheṣv-amameṣu* ... Msl: ... *asvāmikeṣu dharmanairātmyena adharmeṣu pudgalanairātmyena amameṣu aparigraheṣu* ... Cp. para. 38, n. 4. **(18)** Msl: *māyālambana°.*

Pāli: *yato ca kho bhikkhave, mātāpitaro ca samnipatitā honti, matā ca utunī hoti, gandhabbo ca paccupaṭṭhito hoti, evaṁ tiṇṇaṁ samnipātā gandhabbassāvakkhanti hoti* (M1:266).

SF: *'ond kyang sa bon rnam par shes pa las kyi zhing la rtend pa sred pa'i rland kyis brlan pa'o| ma rig pa'i ltad kyis btab pa| skye ba na ma'i mngal de dang der mying dang gzugs kyi myi gu mngon bar 'grub ste| mying dang gzugs kyi myi gu de yang bdag gis ma byas| pha rold kyis ma byas| gnyis kas ma byas| dbang pos ma spruld| dus kyis ma bsgyurd| rang bzhin las ma byung| byed pa la rag las pa ma yin| rgyu myed pa las kyang ma skyes te| pha dang ma phrad pa dang dus dang ldan ba dang rkyend gzhan yang tshogs pa na| bdag po myed pa'i chos bdagi myed pa 'dzind pa myed pa| nam ka dang mtshungs pa sgyu ma'i mtshan nyid dang rang bzhin dag la rgyu dang rkyend ma tshang ba myed pa'i phyir| skye ba'i gnas nyid mtshams sbyor ba| ma'i mngal de dang der myong ba dang ldan ba'i sa bon rnam par shes pa mying dang gzugs kyi myi gu mngon bar sgrub bo||*

35. Furthermore, [1] eye-consciousness arises by way of five principles. What five? Namely, conditioned by eye, form, light, space, and appropriate attention,[2] eye-consciousness arises. Therein, the eye performs the function of being the basis of eye-consciousness. Form performs the function of being the object. Light performs the function of illumination. Space performs the function of uncovering.[3] Appropriate attention performs the function of reflection.[4] Without these conditions, eye-consciousness does not arise. But if the subjective eye-entrance is not deficient, and form, light, space and appropriate attention are not deficient, then, from the conjunction of all these, eye-consciousness arises.[5] Therein, it does not occur to the eye, "I perform the function of being the basis[6] of eye-consciousness". Nor does it occur to form, "I perform the function of being the object of eye-consciousness". Nor does it occur to light, "I perform the function of the illumination of eye-consciousness." Nor does it occur to space, "I perform the uncovering-function of eye-consciousness". Nor does it occur to appropriate attention, "I perform the reflection-function of eye-consciousness". Nor does it occur to eye-consciousness, "I am born by way of these conditions". But still, there being these conditions, the arising of eye-consciousness occurs because of their conjunction. Thus, a corresponding (analysis) of the remaining (sense) faculties should be done.[7]

Mp. 567 Ss. 225 Msl. 113

35.[8] tadyathā pañcabhiḥ kāraṇaiś-cakṣurvijñānam-utpadyate| katamaiḥ pañcabhih, yaduta[9] cakṣuḥ [10] pratītya rūpaṁ cālokaṁ cākāśaṁ [11] tajjamanasikāraṁ ca[12] pratītyotpadyate-cakṣurvijñānaṁ| tatra cakṣurvijñānasya cakṣurāśrayakṛtyaṁ karoti, rūpam-ālambanakṛtyaṁ[13] karoti, āloko 'vabhāsakṛtyaṁ karoti, ākāśam-anāvaraṇakṛtyaṁ karoti, tajjamanasikāraḥ samanvāhāraṇakṛtyaṁ[14] karoti|| asatām-eṣāṁ pratyayānāṁ[15] cakṣurvijñānaṁ notpadyate| yadā tu[16] cakṣurādhyātmikam-āyatanam-avikalaṁ bhavati, evaṁ rūpālokākāśatajjamanasikārāś-cāvikalā bhavanti| tataḥ sarveṣaṁ[17] samavāyāc-cakṣurvijñānam-utpadyate[18]|| tatra[19] cakṣuṣo naivaṁ bhavaty-ahaṁ cakṣurvijñānasyāśrayakṛtyaṁ karomīti| evaṁ[20] rūpasyāpi naivaṁ bhavaty-ahaṁ cakṣurvijñānasyālambanakṛtyaṁ[21] karomīti| ālokasyāpi naivaṁ bhavaty-ahaṁ cakṣurvijñānasyāvabhāsakṛtyaṁ[22] karomīti| ākāśasyāpi naivaṁ bhavaty-ahaṁ cakṣurvijñānasyānāvaraṇakṛtyaṁ karomīti| tajjamanasikārasyāpi naivaṁ bhavaty-ahaṁ cakṣurvijñānasya samanvāhāraṇakṛtyaṁ[23] karomīti| cakṣurvijñānasyāpi naivaṁ bhavaty-aham-ebhiḥ pratyayair-janitam-iti[24]|| atha ca satām-eṣaṁ pratyayānāṁ samavāyāc-cakṣurvijñānasyotpattir-bhavati||[25] evaṁ śeṣāṇām-indriyāṇāṁ yathāyogaṁ karaṇīyaṁ[26]||

35. 'di lta ste| mig gi rnam par shes pa ni rgyu lngas 'byung ste| lnga gang zhe na| mig la rten pa dang| gzugs dang| snang ba dang| nam mkha' dang| de skyed pa'i yid la byed pa la yang rten nas mig gi rnam par shes pa 'byung ngo|| de la mig ni mig gi rnam par shes

pa'i rten gi bya ba byed do|| gzugs ni mig gi rnam par shes pa'i dmigs pa'i bya ba byed do|| snang ba ni mngon pa'i bya ba byed do|| nam mkha' ni mi sgrib pa'i bya ba byed do|| de dang 'byung ba yid la byed pa ni bsam pa'i bya ba byed do| rkyen de dag med na mig gi rnam par shes pa 'byung bar mi 'gyur gyi| gang gi tshe nang gi skye mched mig ma tshang bar ma gyur la| de bzhin du gzugs dang| snang ba dang| nam mkha' dang| de dang 'byung ba yid la byed pa dag ma tshang bar ma gyur te| thams cad 'dus pa de las mig gi rnam par shes pa 'byung bar 'gyur ro|| de la mig ni 'di snyam du bdag gis mig gi rnam par shes pa'i rten gyi bya ba bya'o snyam du mi sems so|| gzugs kyang 'di snyam du bdag gis mig gi rnam par shes pa'i dmigs pa'i bya ba bya'o snyam du mi sems so|| snang ba yang 'di snyam du bdag gis mig gi rnam par shes pa'i mngon pa'i bya ba bya'o snyam du mi sems so|| nam mkha' yang 'di snyam du bdag gis mig gi rnam par shes pa'i mi sgrib pa'i bya ba bya'o snyam du mi sems so|| de dang 'byung ba'i yid la byed pa yang 'di snyam du bdag gis mig gi rnam par shes pa'i bsam pa'i bya ba bya'o snyam du mi sems so|| mig gi rnam par shes pa yang 'di snyam du bdag ni rkyen 'di dag gis bskyed do snyam du mi sems te| 'on kyang rkyen 'di dag yod pa las mig gi rnam par shes pa skye bar 'gyur ro|| de bzhin du dbang po lhag ma rnams kyang ci rigs su sbyar ro||

(1) C. inserts: Venerable Śāriputra. **(2)** *Tajjamanasikāra* = lit. "making in the mind (which is) born from that". **(3)** *anāvaraṇa*. C: Empty space makes no obstacle. Cp. para. 13, n.3. **(4)** *samanvāhāraṇa*, lit. "bringing well along". C: Appropriate attention arises, and therefore eye-consciousness is born. **(5)** C. omits sentence. **(6)** C: It does not occur to eye consciousness (*sic*), "I can function as the bodily basis". **(7)** For last sentence, C: Thus, visual consciousness, valid and mistaken, is produced by many conditions together. Like this, each of these (sense) bases produces consciousness, and is similarly explained. **(8)** Bp: *peyālam*, omitting para. 35. Msl. inserts: *peyālam, peyālaśabdena sāvaśeṣaṁ nirdiśati*||, but includes para. 35. **(9)** Ss., Msl. omit. **(10)** Ss., Msl: *cakṣuś-ca*. **(11)** Msl. inserts *ca*. **(12)** Ss: *tajjaṁ ca manasi°*. **(13)** Ss: *°ārambaṇakṛtyaṁ*. **(14)** Ss: *°āhārakṛtyaṁ*. **(15)** Ss: *asatsv-eṣu pratyayeṣu*. Msl: *asatsu pratyayeṣu*. **(16)** Ss:, Msl. omit. **(17)** Ss: *sarva-*. **(18)** Ss., Msl: *°vijñānasyotpattir-bhavati*|. **(19)** Msl: *tatrāpi*. **(20)** Ss., Msl. omit. **(21)** Ss. *°ārambaṇakṛtyaṁ*. Msl: *°avālambana°*. **(22)** Ss: *aham-avabhāsa°*. **(23)** Ss: *samanvāhārakṛtyaṁ*. **(24)** Ss: *°janita iti*|. Msl: *pratyayasamavāyair-janita iti*|. **(25)** Ss: *atha ca punaḥ satsv-eṣu pratyayeṣu cakṣur ... bhavati prādurbhavaḥ*|. Msl: *atha ca satsu pratyayeṣu cakṣur ... otpattiḥ prādurbhāvo bhavati*|. **(26)** Ss., Msl: *kartavyam*||.

Pāli: *yato ca kho āvuso ajjhattikañceva cakkhuṁ aparibhinnaṁ hoti bāhirā ca rūpā āpāthaṁ āgacchanti tajjo ca samannāhāro hoti, evaṁ tajjassa viññāṇabhāgassa pātubhāvo hoti* (M1:190, cp. M1: 111). (Immediately following is: *yo paṭiccasamuppādaṁ passati so dhammaṁ passati* ... M1:191).

SF: *'di lta ste myig gi rnam par shes pa ni lnga'i phyir skye'o| lnga gang zhe na myig la brtend pa dang| gzugs dang| snang ba dang| nam mkha dang| de skyed pa yid la byed pa la yang brtend nas myig gi rnam par shes pa skye'o| ...*

36. Therein,[1] there is nothing whatsoever that transmigrates from this world to another world. There is (only) the appearance of the fruit of karma, because of the non-deficiency of causes and conditions.[2] It is, monks,[3] like the reflection of a face seen in a well-polished mirror.[4] [5]No face transmigrates into the mirror, but there is the appearance of a face because of the non-deficiency of causes and conditions. Thus there is nothing departed from this world, nor arisen elsewhere. There is (only) the appearance of the fruit of karma, because of the non-deficiency of causes and conditions.[5]

Mp. 568 Ss. 225 Bp. 481 Msl. 113

36. tatra na[6] kaścid-dharmo 'smāl-lokāt-paralokaṁ saṁkrāmati| [7] asti ca karmaphalapratiivijñaptir-hetupratyayānām-avaikalyāt||[8] tadyathā bhikṣavaḥ[9] supariśuddha ādarṣamaṇḍale mukhapratibimbakaṁ dṛśyate| na ca tatrādarśamaṇḍale mukhaṁ saṁkrāmati| asti ca mukhaprativijñaptir-hetupratyayānām-avaikalyāt|| evam-asmāl-lokān-na kaścic-cyuto nāpy-anyatropapannaḥ| asti ca karmaphalaprajñaptir-hetupratyayānām-avaikalyāt||

36. de la chos gang yang 'jig rten 'di nas 'jig rten pha rol du mi 'pho mod kyi| rgyu dang rkyen ma tshang ba med pa'i phyir las kyi 'bras bur mngon pa yang yod do|| 'di lta ste| dber na rab tu phyis pa'i me long gi dkyil 'khor la bzhin gyi gzugs brnyan snang ba yang bzhin me long gi dkyil 'khor du ma 'phos mod kyi| rgyu dang rkyen ma tshang ba med pa'i phyir bzhin du mngon pa yang yod do|| de bzhin du 'di nas kyang su yang shi 'phos pa med la gzhan du yang ma skyes te| rgyu dang rkyen rnams ma tshang ba med pa'i phyir las kyi 'bras bu mngon pa yang yod do||

(1) C: Again, Śāriputra. **(2)** C: But (if) the fruit of karma is substantial and many conditions harmonize, then (there is) birth. **(3)** C: Śāriputra. **(4)** See Conze, *Buddhist Thought*, p. 222; *Buddhist Texts*, p. 16. See also *Mahāyānasaṁgraha*, Lamotte trans., pp. 93-5; *Lankāvatara*, Suzuki trans., p. 278. **(5-5)** C: Mirror and face are in different places, but (even though there is) no going and coming, they are seen in the same place. **(6)** Bp: *na tatra*. Msl: *tatra pratītyasamutpāde na*. **(7)** Msl. inserts: *iti śāśvatāntaniṣedhaḥ*. **(8)** Bp: *°phalam-asti ca vijñaptir-hetu°* ... *avaikalyāt| peyālaṁ*|, omitting rest of para. 36 and para. 37. Ss. omits same without ellipsis. Msl: *peyālam*|, omitting as Bp. and Ss. **(9)** T. omits.

SF: ... *('di nas 'ji)g rten pha roldu myi 'pho mod kyi ... (ma 'phos) mod kyi rgyu dang rkyend ma tshan ba myed (pa'i phyir) ...*

37. It is, (monks,)* like the moon-disk which wanders 4,000 leagues above,[1] and yet again the moon's reflection is seen in a small pool of water. It does not depart from its station (in the sky)* above and transmigrate into the small pool of water, but there is the appearance of the moon-disk, because of the non-deficiency of causes and conditions. Thus, there is nothing departed from this world, nor arisen elsewhere. (There is (only) the appearance of the fruit of karma, because of the non-deficiency of causes and conditions,)*[2]

Mp. 568
37.[3] tadyathā (bhikṣavaś) candramaṇḍalaṁ catvāriṁśad-yojana-śatam-ūrdhvaṁ[4] vrajati| atha ca punaḥ paritte 'py-udakabhājane candrasya pratibimbaṁ dṛṣyate| na ca tasmāt-sthānād-ūrdhvaṁ-(nabhasaś)cyutaṁ paritte udakasya bhājane saṁkrāntaṁ bhavati| asti ca candramaṇḍalaprativijñaptir-hetupratyayānām-avaikalyāt| (evam-asmāl-lokān-na kaścic-cyuto, nāpy-anyatropapannaḥ| asti ca karmaphalaprativijñaptir-hetupratyayānām-avaikalyāt||)

37. 'di lta ste| dper na zla ba'i dkyil 'khor ni dpag tshad bzhi khri nyis stong nas 'gro ste| 'on kyang snod chung du chus gang bar zla ba'i dkyil 'khor gyi gzugs brnyan snang ba yang zla ba'i dkyil 'khor ni gnas de nas ma 'phos te| snod chung du chus gang ba'i nang du song ba yang med mod kyi| rgyu dang rkyen ma tshang ba med pa'i phyir zla ba'i dkyil 'khor du mngon pa yang yod do|| de bzhin du 'di nas kyang su yang shi 'phos pa med la gzhan du yang ma skyes mod kyi| rgyu dang rkyen rnams ma tshang ba med pa'i phyir las kyi 'bras bu mngon pa yang yod do||

(1) T. and C: 42,000 leagues (*yojana* = *dpag tshad*). **(2)** For para. 37, C: Again Śāriputra, (it is) as the moon (in) the beautiful sky 42,000 leagues above the earth. The water flows below and the moon shines above. Although its mysterious image is single, (its) reflection appears in many waters. The moon's body does not descend and the water's substance does not rise. Thus, Śāriputra, creatures do not go from this world to an after-world, or from an after-world again to this world. But there are the fruits of karma (and) the outcomes of causes and conditions which cannot be diminished. **(3)** Only Mp. and T. include para. 37. **(4)** T: 42,000 *yojanāḥ*.

SF: *('di lta ste) dper na zla ba'i dkyil 'khord ni ... (chus) gang ba'i nang du song ba yang myed mod (kyi ... las) kyi 'bras bur mngon ba yang yo(d) do|*

38. Just as when there is fuel as a condition, fire burns, (and) if fuel is deficient, it does not burn; even so does the consciousness-seed, born of karma-defilements, cause the sprout of name-and-form to develop here and there in the entrances of arising, through rebirth in a mother's womb, in (relation to) things (which are) not governed, not "mine", not possessed, (not opposed,)* like space, of the nature of the marks of illusion, due to the non-deficiency of causes and conditions. Thus is the conditional relation in subjective conditioned arising to be seen.[1]

Mp. 568 Ss. 226 Bp. 482 Msl. 113

38. tadyathāgnir-upādānapratyaye sati jvalati, upādānavaikalyān-na jvalati|[2] evameva [3] karmakleśajanitaṁ vijñānabījaṁ tatratatropapattyāyatanapratisaṁdhau mātuḥ kukṣau nāmarūpāṅkuram-abhinirvartayati| asvāmikeṣu [4]dharmeṣv-amameṣu aparigraheṣu-(apratyarthikeṣu) ākāśasameṣu māyālakṣaṇasvabhāveṣu[4] hetu-pratyayānām-avaikalyāt|| evam-ādhyātmikasya pratītyasamutpādasya pratyayopanibandho draṣṭavyaḥ||[5]

38. 'di lta ste| dper na me ni rgyu dang rkyen ma tshang na mi 'bar gyi| rgyu dang rkyen 'tshogs pa las 'bar ro|| de bzhin du bdag po med pa'i chos| bdag gi med pa| 'dsin pa med pa| nam mkha' dang mtshungs pa| sgyu ma'i mtshan nyid kyi rang bzhin dag la rgyu dang rkyen rnams ma tshang ba med pa'i phyir skye ba'i gnas nyid mtshams syor ba ma'i mngal de dang der sa bon rnam par shes pa las dang nyon mongs pa rnams kyis bskyed pa ming dang gzugs kyi myu gu mngon par 'grub ste| de ltar nang gi rten cing 'brel bar 'byung ba rkyen dang 'brel bar blta'o||

(1) For para. 38, C: Again, Venerable Śāriputra, (it is) as (when) fire has fuel it burns, and when the fuel is gone it stops. Likewise karma bondage produces consciousness everywhere (in) all realms. (It) can produce the result, name-and-form, (which is) not self, not a master, not a recipient, like empty space, like summer heat (mirages), like an illusion, like a dream, not having substance. Yet its virtuous and evil causes and conditions, fruits and results follow *karma* undiminished. (2) Bp., Msl: *yathā agnir-upādanavaikalyān-na jvalati, upādānāvaikalyāc-ca jvalati.* T: *(tad)yathāgnir hetupratyayavaikalyān na jvalati, hetupratyayāvaikalyāc-ca jvalati|.* (3) Mp. inserts: *bhikṣavaḥ.* (4-4) Following Ss. Bp. as Ss., but observes *yan sandhi* and omits *ākāśasameṣu.* T. omits *apratyarthikeṣu.* Mp: *dharmeṣvaparigraheṣu māyālakṣaṇasvabhāveṣv-amameṣu kṛtrimeṣu.* Msl: *asvāmikeṣu adharmeṣu ... °svabhāveṣu.* Cp. para. 34, n. 17. (5) Mp., Ss. omit sentence.

Pāli: *seyyathā pi bhikkhave yañyadeva paccayaṁ paṭicca aggi jalati tena teneva saṅkhaṁ gacchati, kaṭṭhañca paṭicca aggi jalati, kaṭṭhaggi teva saṅkhaṁ gacchati, sakalikañca paṭicca aggi jalati ... tiṇañca ... gomayañca ... thusañca ... saṅkārañca paṭicca aggi jalati, saṅkāraggi tveva saṅkhaṁ gacchati, evameva kho bhikkhave yaññadeva paccayaṁ paṭicca uppajati viññāṇaṁ tena teneva saṅkhaṁ gacchati, cakkhuñca paṭicca rūpe ca uppajjati viññāṇaṁ, cakkhuviññāṇantveva saṅkhaṁ gacchati ... manoviññāṇantveva saṅkhaṁ gacchati* (M1:259-260, cp. S2:86).

SF: *'(di lta ste|* ... nam mkh)a dang mtshungs pa sgyu ma'i mtshan nyid dang rang bzhin dag la| rgyu dang (rkyend) ma tshan ba myed pa'i phyir skye ba'i gnas nyid mtshams sbyor ba| ma'i mngal de dang der sa bon rnam par shes pa las dang nyon (mongs ... mying dang gzugs) kyi myi gu mngon bar sgrub ste| de ltar nang gi rtend cing '(brel)d par 'byung bai rkyend 'breld par bltao||

39. Furthermore, subjective conditioned arising is to be seen according to five principles.[1] What five? Not as eternity, not as annihilation, not as transmigration, as the development of a large fruit from a small cause, and as (a result) bound to be similar to that (its cause).

Mp. 569 Ss. 226 Bp. 482 Msl. 114
39. tatrādhyātmikaḥ[2] pratītyasamutpādaḥ pañcabhiḥ kāraṇir-draṣṭavyaḥ| katamaiḥ pañcabhiḥ| [3] na śāśvatato nocchedato na saṁkrāntitaḥ parīttahetuto-vipulaphalābhinirvṛttitaḥ[4] tat-sadṛṣānuprabandhataś-ceti||

39. de la nang gi rten cing 'brel bar 'byung ba rnam pa lngar blta ste| lnga gang zhe na| rtag par ma yin pa dang| chad par ma yin pa dang| 'pho bar ma yin pa dang| rgyu chung du las 'bras bu chen po 'byung ba dang| de dang 'dra ba'i rgyud du'o||

(1) See para. 15, n. 1-5. For para. 39, C: Again, Venerable Śāriputra, conditioned arising also arises from five causes and conditions. (2) Ss: *tannādhy°* (3) Msl. inserts: *yaduta.* (4) Mp: *°hetuvipula°.*

SF: *de la nang gi rtend cing 'breld par 'byung ba lnga'i phyir blta ste| lnga gang zhe na| ... ('pho bar) ma yin ba dang| rgyu chungu las 'bras bu chen po 'byung ba da(ng| de) dang 'dra ba'i rgyud du'o|*

40. How (is it to be seen) as "not eternity"? Because the aggregates on the edge of death are one thing, and the aggregates sharing arising are another. The aggregates on the edge of death are not (identical to) those sharing arising. But still, the aggregates on the edge of death cease, (and) the aggregates sharing arising become manifest. Therefore eternity is not (the case).[1]

Mp. 569 Ss. 226 Bp. 482 Msl. 114
40. kathaṁ na śāśvatato, yasmād-anye māraṇāntikāḥ skandhā anye aupapattyaṁśikāḥ skandhāḥ[2]| na tu ya eva māraṇāntikāḥ skandhās-ta evaupapattyaṁśikāḥ[3] [4]api tu māraṇāntikāḥ[5] skandhā nirudhyante[6]| aupapattyaṁśikāḥ skandhāḥ[7] prādurbhavanti|[4] ato [8] na śāśvatataḥ||

40. ji ltar rtag par ma yin zhe na| gang gi phyir tha ma'i 'chi ba'i phung po rnams kyang gzhan la| skye ba'i char gtogs pa rnams kyang gzhan te| tha ma 'chi ba'i phung po gang yin pa de nyid skye ba'i char gtogs pa rnams ma yin gyi| tha ma'i 'chi ba'i phung po rnams kyang 'gag la skye ba'i char gtogs pa'i phung po rnams kyang 'byung bas de'i phyir rtag par ma yin no||

(1) For para. 40, C: Why not eternal? One aggregate perishes, another arises. (That which) perishes is not what then arises. That which arises is not that which perishes. Therefore (it is) called not eternal. **(2)** Ss. omits. Bp., Msl: *skandhāḥ prādurbhavanti.* **(3)** Ss. adds: *skandhāḥ.* Bp. adds: *prādurbhavante.* Msl. adds: *skandhāḥ prādurbhavantīti na|* **(4-4)** Bp., Msl. omit. **(5)** Ss: °*kāś-ca.* **(6)** Ss: *nirudhyamānā.* **(7)** Ss: °*dhāś-ca.* **(8)** Msl. inserts *hetor.*

SF: *ji ltar rtag par ma yin zhe na| gang gi phyir tha ma'i 'chi ba'i phung po rnams kyang gzhan la skye ba'i char (gtogs ... tha ma 'chi ba)'i phung po gang yin ba de nyid skye ba'i char gtogs pa rnams ma yin gyi tha ma 'chi ba'i phung po rnams kyang 'gag la| skye ba'i char gtogs pa'i phung po rnams kyang 'byung ...*

41. How (is it to be seen) as "not annihilation"? The aggregates sharing arising do not become manifest from the previous cessation of the aggregates on the edge of death, nor without this cessation. But still, the aggregates on the edge of death cease, and at just that time, the aggregates sharing arising become manifest, like the beam of a scale rocking to and fro. Therefore, annihilation is not (the case).[1]

Mp. 569 Ss. 226 Bp. 482 Msl. 114
41. kathaṁ nocchedataḥ|[2] na ca [3]pūrva-niruddheṣu māraṇāntikeṣu[3] skandheṣu aupapattyaṁśikāḥ skandhāḥ prādurbhavanti nāpy-aniruddheṣu| api tu māraṇāntikāḥ[4] skandhā nirudhyante, [5]tasminneva ca samaya[5] [6]aupapattyaṁśikāḥ skandhāḥ[6] prādurbhavanti tulādaṇḍonnāmāvanāmavat[7]| ato nocchedataḥ||

41. ji ltar chad par ma yin zhe na| tha ma'i 'chi ba'i phung po rnams sngon 'gags pa las skye ba'i char gtogs pa'i phung po rnams

'byung ba ma yin| ma 'gags pa las kyang ma yin gyi| tha ma'i 'chi ba'i phung po rnams 'gags la| de nyid kyi tshe skye ba'i char gtogs pa'i phung po rnams srang mda'i mtho dman bzhin 'byung bar 'gyur te| de'i phyir chad par ma yin no||

(1) For para. 41, C: Why not annihilation? Like a scale rocking, this perishes and that arises. Therefore (it is) not annihilation, known and seen as it really is. **(2)** Mp. omits. Msl: *kathaṁ punar-no°*. **(3-3)** Ss: *niruddheṣu*.. **(4)** Ss: *°kaś-ca*. **(5-5)** Ss. omits. Msl: *°samaye*. **(6-6)** Ss: *°kāś-ca (prādur°)*. Msl: *°kaś-ca skandāḥ punar-bhavanti, (prādur°)*. **(7)** Mp. adds: *candrabimbapratibimbavat*.

SF: *(ji ltar chad par ma) yin zhe na| tha ma 'chi ba'i phung po rnams 'gags pa las| skye ba'i char gtogs pa'i phung po rnams 'byung ba ma yin| ma 'gags pa las kyang ma yin gyi| tha ma 'chi ba'i phung (po) ...*

42. How (is it to be seen) as "not transmigration"? Dissimilar species cause birth to develop in a common category of birth. Therefore transmigration is not (the case).[1]

Mp. 569 Ss. 226 Bp. 483 Msl. 114
42. Kathaṁ na saṁkrāntitaḥ|[2] visadṛṣāḥ sattvanikāyāḥ sabhāgatāyāṁ (satyām) jātyāṁ jātim-abhinirvartayanti|[3] ato na saṁkrāntitaḥ||

42. ji ltar 'pho bar ma yin zhe na| sems can gyi ris mi 'dra ba nas skal ba mnyam pa'i skye bar skye ba mngon par sgrub pas de'i phyir 'pho bar ma yin no||

(1) For para. 42, C: Why not coming or going? The seed does not go to the sprout, and the sprout does not come and take the seed's place. This is why (it is) without (transmigration) from here to there. **(2)** Ss. omits. Msl. adds *iti*. **(3)** Ss., Bp: *visadṛśātsattvanikāyādvisabhāgāḥ skandā jātyantare'bhinirvartante|*. Msl. as Ss. and Bp., but *°jatyantareṣv-abhi°*. T: *viśadṛśātsattvanikāyāt sabhāgā jātir-abhinirvartate* (VP), probably the best reading.

43. How (is it to be seen) as "the development of a large fruit from a small cause"? A small deed (karma) is done, and a large resultant fruit is experienced. Therefore, "the development of a large fruit from a small cause" is (the case).[1]

Mp. 569 Ss. 226 Bp. 483 Msl. 114
43. kathaṁ parīttahetuto vipulaphalābhinirvṛttitaḥ|[2] parīttaṁ karma kriyate vipulaḥ phalavipāko'nubhūyate| ataḥ parīttahetuto vipulaphalābhinirvṛttitaḥ[3]||

43. ji ltar rgyu chung du las 'bras bu chen po 'byung zhe na| las chung du byas pa las 'bras bu chen po'i rnam par smin pa myong ste| de'i phyir rgyu chung du las 'bras bu chen po mngon par 'grub bo||

(1) C. has only: Truly, few seeds can produce many fruits. **(2)** Ss. omits. **(3)** Ss: *°vṛttiḥ*.

44. How (is it to be seen) as "(an effect) bound to be similar to that (its cause)". [1]Whatever type of deed (karma) is done, that (same) type of result is experienced. There, (the effect) is bound to be similar to that (its cause). (Thus is subjective conditioned arising to be seen in five ways.)*[1]

Mp. 569 Ss. 227 Bp. 483 Msl. 114
44. kathaṁ tat-sadṛśānuprabandhataḥ|[2] yathā-vedanīyaṁ karma kriyate tathā-vedanīyo vipāko'nubhūyate| atas-tat-sadṛśānuprabandhataḥ[3]|| (evam-ādhyātmikaḥ pratītyasamutpādaḥ pañcabhir-draṣṭavyaḥ||)[4]

44. ji ltar myong bar 'gyur ba'i las byas pa de ltar myong bar 'gyur ba'i rnam par smin pa myong pas de'i phyir de dang 'dra ba'i rgyud du'o||

(1-1) C: If non-virtuous, the cause produces a non-virtuous fruit. If virtuous ... virtuous fruit. This is why it is said: "Similar and continuous (things) are produced". **(2)** Ss. omits. **(3)** Ss., Msl: °*taś-ceti.* Mp: °*anubandhataś-ceti vistaraḥ*, but has paras. 45-46 on pp. 593-4. **(4)** All but Bp. omit. Bp. citation ends here with: °*vya iti vistaraḥ*.

45. Whoever, Venerable Śāriputra, with perfect wisdom, sees this conditioned arising, perfectly set forth by the Lord, as it actually is: always and ever without soul, devoid of soul, truly undistorted, unborn, not become, not made, not compounded, unobstructed, unobscured, glorious, fearless, ungraspable, inexhaustable and by nature never stilled, (whoever) sees it well and fully as unreal, as vanity, void, unsubstantial, as a sickness, a boil, a dart,[1] as dangerous, impermanent, suffering, as empty and without self; such a one does not reflect upon the past (thinking): "Was I in the past, or was I not? What was I in the past? How was I in the past?" Nor again does he reflect upon the future (thinking): "Will I be in the future, or will I not be? What will I be in the future? How will I be in the future?" Nor again does he reflect upon the present (thinking): "What is this? How is this? Being what, what will we become? Where does this being come from? Where will it go when departed from here?"[2]

Mp. 593 Ss. 227 Msl. 114
45. [3]yaḥ kaścid-bhadanta śāriputremaṁ pratītyasamutpādaṁ bhagavatā samyak praṇītam-evaṁ[3] yathābhūtaṁ samyakprajñayā satatasamitam-ajīvaṁ nirjīvaṁ[4] yathāvad-aviparītam-ajātam-abhūtam-akṛtam-asaṁskṛtam-apratigham-anāvaraṇaṁ[5] śivam-abhayam-anāhāryam[6]-avyayam-avyupaśamasvabhāvaṁ paśyati, asatas-tucchato[7] ṛktato[8] 'sārato [9]rogato gaṇḍataḥ śalyato[9] 'ghato[10] 'nityato duḥkhataḥ śūnyato [11]'nātmataś-ca samanupaśyati,[11] sa na[12] pūrvāntaṁ pratisarati| kim nv-aham-abhūvam-atīte[13] 'dhvani āhosvin-nābhūvam-atīte 'dhvani, ko nv-aham-abhūvamatīte 'dhvani, [14]kathaṁ nv-aham-abhūvam-atīte 'dhvani|[14] aparāntaṁ vā punar-na pratisarati, kiṁ [15]nv-ahaṁ bhaviṣyāmy-anāgate[15] 'dhvani āhosvin-na bhaviṣyāmy-anāgate[16] 'dhvani, ko nu[17] [18]bhaviṣyāmy-anāgate 'dhvani, kathaṁ nu bhaviṣyāmy-anāgate 'dhvani[18]| pratyutpannaṁ vā punar-na pratisarati, kiṁ nv-idaṁ[19] kathaṁ

nv-idam[19] ke santaḥ ke bhaviṣyāmaḥ,[20] ayaṁ sattvaḥ kuta āgatah|
sa itaś-cyutaḥ kutra gamiṣyatīti||

45. btsun pa shā ri'i bu rten cing 'brel bar 'byung ba bcom ldan 'das kyis yang dag par gsungs pa 'di gang la la zhig gis yang dag pa'i shes rab kyis de ltar yang dag pa ji lta bu bzhin du rtag par rgyun du srog med pa dang| srog dang bral ba dang| ji lta bu nyid dang| ma nor ba dang| ma skyes pa dang| ma byung ba dang| ma byas pa dang| 'dus ma byas pa dang| thogs pa med pa dang| dmigs pa med pa dang| zhi ba dang| 'jigs pa med pa dang| mi 'phrogs pa dang| zad pa med pa dang| rnam par zhi ba ma yin pa'i rang bzhin du mthong ba dang| med pa dang| gsog dang| gsob dang| snying po med pa dang| nad dang 'bras dang| zug rngu dang| sdig pa dang| mi rtag pa dang| sdug bsngal ba dang| stong ba dang| bdag med par yang dag par rjes su mthong ba de ni ci bdag 'das pa'i dus na 'byung ba zhig gam| 'on te bdag 'das pa'i dus na mi 'byung ba zhig| bdag 'das pa'i dus na cir gyur pa zhig| bdag 'das pa'i dus na ji lta bur gyur ba zhig gu snyam du sngon gi mtha' la mi rtog go|| ci ma 'ongs pa'i dus na 'byung bar 'gyur ram| 'on te ma 'ongs pa'i dus na 'byung bar mi 'gyur| ma 'ongs pa'i dus na cir 'gyur| ma 'ongs pa'i dus na ji lta bu zhig tu 'gyur snyam du phyi ma'i mtha' la mi rtog go|| 'di ci zhig| 'di ji lta bu zhig| ci zhig yod| cir 'gyur| sems can 'di dag gang nas 'ongs| 'di nas shi 'phos nas gang du 'gro bar 'gyur shes de ltar byung ba la yang mi rtog go||

(1) Cp. M2:230; Vsm. 355. **(2)** See M1:265; S2:26 on these "fruitless ponderings". For para. 45, C: Again, Śāriputra, as the Buddha said,"Being able to perceive conditioned arising is called right view. If one rightly perceives conditioned arising, there do not arise thoughts about the existence of the past body and there do not arise thoughts about the non-existence of the body in the future, (or thoughts such as:) "These beings, from where have they come? Where do they go?" **(3-3)** Mp. has only: *ya imaṁ pratītyasamutpādam.* **(4)** Mp. omits. **(5)** Msl: *°aparītaṁ ... asaṁskṛtaṁ apratimaṁ anāvaraṇaṁ.* **(6)** Ss., Msl: *°ahāryaṁ ...* **(7)** Ss: *asatyatas-tucchata* Msl: *asatyato'saktataḥ (asārato ...).* **(8)** Msl. omits. **(9-9)** Ss. omits. **(10)** Msl. omits. **(11-11)** Mp: *'nātmataḥ,* (na sa ...). **(12)** Mp: *na sa.* **(13)** Ss., Msl: omit *nu* **(14-14)** Ss., Msl. omit. **(15-15)** Ss. omits *ahaṁ.* Msl: *bhaviṣyāmy-aham-anāgate.* **(16)** Msl: as n. 15. **(17)** Msl: *nv-ahaṁ.* **(18-18)** Ss., Msl: *bhaviṣyāmīti* only. **(19)** Ss: *°svid-idam.* **(20)** Ss., Msl: *°ṣyāma iti||*, ending citations.

Pāli: *ye pi hi koci bhikkhave yaṁ loke piyarūpaṁ sātarūpaṁ taṁ aniccato ... dukkhato ... anattato ... rogato ... bhayato passanti, te taṇhaṁ pajahanti* (S2:112). *yato kho bhikkhave ariyasāvakassa ayañca paṭiccasamuppādo ime ca paṭiccasamuppannā dhammā yathābhutaṁ sammāpaññāya sudiṭṭha hoti. so vata pubbantaṁ vā paṭidhāvissati, ahosiṁ nu khvāhaṁ atītamaddhānaṁ, na nu kho ahosiṁ atītamaddhānaṁ, kiṁ nu kho ahosiṁ atītamaddhānaṁ, kiṁ nu kho ahosiṁ atītamaddhānam, kathaṁ nu kho ahosiṁ atītamaddhānaṁ, kiṁ hutvā kiṁ ahosiṁ nu khvāhaṁ atītamaddhānanti. aparantaṁ vā upadhāvissati ... kiṁ hutvā kiṁ bhavissāmi nu khvāhaṁ anāgatamaddhānanti. etarahi vā paccuppannamaddhānaṁ ajjhattaṁ kathaṁkathī bhavissati, ahaṁ nu khosmi, na nu khosmi, kiṁ nu khosmi, kathaṁ nu khosmi. ahaṁ nu kho satto kuto āgato so kuhiṁgāmī bhavissati ti. netaṁ ṭhānaṁ vijjati* (S2:26-7, cp. M1:8; M1:265).

46. Whatever dogmas[1] the common world's ascetics and priests hold, that is to say, (dogmas) related to: belief in self, [belief in a "being"] belief in soul, [belief in a "person"] rites and rituals,[2] these (dogmas) were abandoned at that time, fully recognized (as false), cut off at the root, withered like the plume of a Taliput palm,[3] *dharmas*[4] never to arise or cease (again) in the future.[5]

Mp. 594

46. yāny-ekeṣāṁ śramaṇabrāhmaṇānāṁ pṛthagloke dṛṣṭigatāni bhaviṣyanti, tadyathā ātmavādapratisaṁyuktāni [sattvavādapratisaṁyuktāni] jīvavādapratisaṁyuktāni [pudgalavādapratisaṁyuktāni] kautukamaṇgalapratisaṁyuktāni,[6] tāny-asya tasmin samaye prahīṇāni bhavanti parijñātāni samucchinnamūlāni tālamastakavad-anābhāsagatā[ni] āyatyām-anutpādānirodhadharmāṇi||

46. 'jig rten na dge sbyong ngam| bram ze dag gi lta bar song ba tha dad pa gang dag yod ba 'di lta ste| bdag tu smra ba dang ldan pa'am| sems can du smra ba dang ldan pa'am| srog tu smra ba dang ldan pa'am| gang zag tu smra ba dang ldan pa'am| dge mtshan dang bkra shis su smra ba dang ldan pa dag kyang rung ste| lhag par g.yo ba dang bral bar g.yo ba de dag de'i tshe na des spangs par 'gyur te| yongs su shes nas rtsa ba nas bcad de| ta la'i mgo bzhin mi snang ba'i rang bzhin du phyis mi skye mi 'gag pa'i chos can du 'gyur ro||

(1) *Drsti* = lit. "views". (2) See the similar rejection of ritual at D1:179; S4: 398; M2:2. (3) The Taliput palm grows to a great height and at maturity produces one huge, green flower out of its plume, and then dies. (4) *Dharma* here could mean simply "thing", but should probably be taken as "mode of conduct or belief". (5) For para. 46, C: If *Śramaṇas, Brāhmaṇas* and worldly men achieve all views: self-view, being-view, life-view, hero-view, auspicious-inauspicious-view. Thus is conditioned arising (*sic.*). Like a *tāla* (fan-palm) tree, severed at the head and unable to grow, self-view will be eliminated. (6) T. inserts: *lhag par g.yo ba dang bral bar g.yo ba*. VP: *vā unmiñjitanimiñjitāni*. NS: *unmiñjitāni nimiñjitāni ca*.

Pāli: *evañhi so bhikkhave mahārukkho uccinnamūlo assa, tālavatthukato anabhāvaṁkato āyatim anuppādadhammo* (S2:88; S3:10, cp. S1:136).

47. [Whosoever, Venerable Śāriputra, thus endowed with patience in the Dharma,[1] understands conditioned arising perfectly, for him the *Tathāgata*, the Noble One, the perfectly, completely enlightened one, endowed with (perfect) wisdom and conduct, the Wellfarer, knower of (all) worlds, incomparable charioteer of men needing taming, teacher of gods and men, the Buddha, the Lord, predicts unsurpassable perfect, complete enlightenment (saying): "He will become a perfect, complete Buddha!"][2]

T. only
47. [yaḥ kaścid bhadanta śāriputra evaṁ dharmakṣāntisaṁpannaḥ pratītyasamutpādam api samyag-avagacchati, tasya tathāgato 'rhaṁ saṁyak-sambuddho vidyācaraṇasampanno sugato lokavid-anuttara-puruṣadamyasārathī śāstā devamanuṣyāṇām buddho bhagavān, samyak-saṁbuddho bhaviṣyatīti, anuttarasamyak-saṁbodhiṁ vyākaroti|]

47. btsun pa shā ri'i bu gang la la chos la bzod pa 'di lta bu dang ldan te| rten cing 'brel bar 'byung ba'di yang dag par khong du chud na de la de bzhin gshegs pa dgra bcom pa yang dag par rdsogs pa'i sangs rgyas rig pa dang zhabs su ldan pa| bde bar gshegs pa| 'jig rten mkhyen pa| skyes bu 'dul ba'i kha lo sgyur ba| bla na med pa lha dang mi rnams kyi ston pa| sangs rgyas bcom ldan 'das kyis yang dag par rdsogs pa'i sangs rgyas su 'gyur ro zhes bla na med pa yang dag par rdsogs pa'i byang chub tu lung bstan to||

(1) *Dharmakṣanti*, but perhaps "belief in the (Buddhist) Dharma", as at D1: 187 where *aññakhantika* = "believer in another (doctrine)". **(2)** For para. 47, C: If one rightly sees conditioned arising, if one gains this understanding, Venerable Śāriputra, and if one of the many beings is patient in the Dharma, of him, the *Tathāgata*, the Noble One, the perfectly, completely enlightened one, the Wellfarer, knower of (all) worlds, the chariot-driving hero, teacher of gods and men, the Buddha, the Lord, proclaims unsurpassable, perfect, complete enlightenment.

Pāli: *manussesu metteyyo nāma bhagavā loke uppajjissati arahaṁ sammāsambuddho vijjācaraṇasampanno sugato lokavidū anuttaro purisadammasārāthi satthā devamanussānaṁ buddho bhagavā* (D3:76).

48a. (According to Mp. 594:) (Then indeed, the Venerable Śāriputra, delighted and joyful at the words of Maitreya *Bodhisattva-mahāsattva*, rose from his seat, and the other monks also departed.)*[1]

Mp. 594
48a. (atha khalv-āyusmān śāriputro maitreyasya bodhisattvasya mahāsattvasya bhāṣitam-abhinandya-modyotthāyāsanāt prakrāntās-te ca bhikṣavaḥ[2]||)

(1) For para. 48, C: Venerable Śāriputra, having heard Maitreya's discourse, was joyful and departed. The gods, *nagas*, *yakṣas*, *gandharvas*, *asuras* and the other great groups prostrated to Maitreya and joyfully departed. (This is) the Rice Scripture spoken by the Buddha. (Cp. para. 48b.) **(2)** Mp: °*kṣava iti*||

Pāli: *idamavoca bhagavā. attamanā te bhikkhū bhagavato bhāsitaṁ abhinandanti* (M1:271, etc.).

48b. (According to T:) [Thus spoke Maitreya *Bodhisattva-mahāsattva*, and the Venerable Śāriputra, together with the world of gods, men, titans and sprites, delighted, rejoiced at the words of Maitreya *Bodhisattva-mahāsattva.*][1]

T. only
48b. [maitreyabodhisattvamahāsattvena evam-uktva, āyuṣmān śāriputraḥ sadevamanuṣyāsuragandharvalokaś-ca pramodyan, maitreyabodhisattvamahāsattvasya bhāsitam abhyanandan||

48b. byang chub sems dpa' sems dpa' chen po byams pas de skad ces smras nas| tshe dang ldan pa shā ri'i bu dang| lha dang| mi dang| lha ma yin dang| dri zar bcas pa'i 'jig rten yi rangs te| byang chub sems dpa' sems dpa' chen po byams pas bshad pa la mngon par bstod do|| 'phags pa sā lu'i ljang pa zhes bya ba theg pa chen po'i mdo rdsogs so||||

Pāli: *imaṁ lokaṁ sadevakaṁ samārakaṁ sabrahmakaṁ sassamaṇabrāhmaṇiṁ pajaṁ sadeva-manussaṁ* ... (D3:76, etc.).